Books are to be returned on or before
the last date below.

2 4 OCT 2003

THE HISTORY
OF
THE FUTURE

Christophe Canto   Odile Faliu

THE HISTORY
OF
THE FUTURE
Images of the 21st Century
Translated by Francis Cowper

Flammarion

CONTENTS

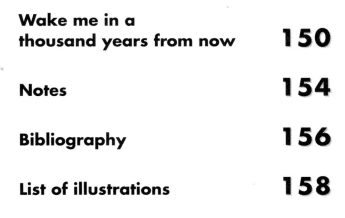

PREFACE

In the days when it was still a fair way off, the year 2000 looked rather different from what we now expect it to be. The future promised tasty meals prepacked in tubes and the delights of climate controlled clothing. In an inoffensive light provided by nuclear energy, we would admire the colours of unbreakable plastic and might appreciate the streamlined contours of the individual jet-cars that people would use to travel to work. Work, of course, would take up no more than two or three hours per day. By the year 2000 sickness was to have disappeared, and poverty would be no more than a bad memory. Pollution would be a thing of the past. Climates would be controlled. Cities would live beneath huge domes. The Sahara would become a green and verdant place, and the Antarctic temperate. This was the world that should have been, with its amazing gadgets on all sides — robots for taking the dog for a walk, or for doing the baby-sitting, 3-D videophone cabins on street corners next to travelator pavements and, every weekend, the pleasure of day-trips to the moon.

Visions such as these, looking forward to an age of perfection, blossomed in their thousands during the period when Western civilisation was in its years of glory, basking in the rays of progress and surfing on growth. However, the spirit of achievement which accompanied the first popular successes of science and big industry was very soon overtaken by a widespread and cogent suspicion that the years to come would have a few surprises in store. Each epoch produced its own model of the future in line with the scientific discoveries and applications of its day; everyone, in their time, imagined what their era allowed them to imagine, and there was an almost unanimous belief in the idea of a constant process of development, advancing problem-free and at a steady pace. The devotees of this school of optimism believed that industrial civilisation was the only model that might one day permit humanity to fulfil its dreams of global harmony; the accomplishment of all this appeared close at hand, and a date suggested itself in the shape of the highly symbolic two thousandth year after the birth of Christ. In the countries which were on the point of declaring themselves as 'developed', the perfect archetype of the future was invented, and it was inaugurated there and then, to the triumphant sound of fanfares and in the glittering splendours of the first World's Fairs.

Among the mythologies of happiness, the prospect of a technological Eden, while it was unable to dissipate the more deeply-rooted doubts, nevertheless appeared credible and acceptable. It was an idealised instant, and people thought it might finally be achieved, given that they had conceived it as being accessible within a few generations. With the immense advances being made, it was reckoned that all this was virtually around the corner. Without a substantial dose of peaceful capitalist development and the associated humanism, without the certainty that human beings would find ways of mastering their destiny, without the belief that humanity was on the threshold of a better world and of being able to take part in its fulfilment, the year 2000, the new Golden Age, the second Renaissance, would never have existed, even on paper. On the threshold of that era — our era — there was a real expectation that all this would come about.

It was to the future that people travelled in order to rediscover that vibrant sense of life that only epic journeys can foster. Among the enthusiasts of the age, a narcissistic concept of destiny became commonplace, and it left its mark in the form of projects for peaceful, trouble-free conquests. Their fulfilment was in sight and a splendid future was taking shape. At this point, given that people were assured that they already occupied the best of all possible places on this earth they then moved to attempting to depict the state in which the world would find itself once it had developed even further, to a point of advanced technological maturity. Writers began to embark on longer-term projections, in a manner that was more intuitive than scientific; they used technology's capacity for perfectibility in order to extrapolate with the greatest verisimilitude they could muster, and, forgetting that science is not infallible, they expected scientists to step forward and supply operating instructions for this projected future. In a kind of ecstasy, they seemed to believe in their creations, as if they represented somehow a rebounding echo of what, sooner or later, would inevitably come to pass. The road to follow, the precurser of things to come.

INTRODUCTION:
THE FUTURE AS HISTORY

1. *The intrepid Georges Méliès conquers the moon. 1902*

The year 2000 has a powerful symbolic value. It stands as the notional end-point of an idealised conception of time. It was one of the major myths of the industrial era, crystallising a series of beliefs, hopes and anxieties — a myth constructed of technological dreams and fantastical achievements. The aim of our book is to bring together written and graphic representations of the future, based on the theme of the year 2000 as it has been evoked in the recent past — an exploration of how this future has been created in the popular imagination.

However, as we now approach the year 2000, the myth begins to pale: it is almost physically present, for time has caught up with it — and here we are, still alive. It is only a matter of time before we enter real history and reality strips these creations, built of a subtle interplay between the possible and the probable and multiple variations in between, of their unreality. They stand now as archaeological remnants that ask to be seen in the context of the past. The future as history is a construction of tales and images from another time.

In examining the creation of this mythic construction, our book offers a selection of

2. *Steam trip in London, or* Hyde Park As It Will Be. *1820*

prefigurations of the twenty-first century, and, more generally, a view of the ways in which the future has been perceived throughout the period of industrial society — principally in the West — in the light of an all-pervasive science which has been active in both organising and explaining the world. Our retrospective history of visions of the future highlights the privileged place occupied by the years 1851-1961. The year 2000 was to offer the prototype of an ideal society in which science and technology would provide the ingredients of human happiness; it provided a symbolic focus for optimistic ideologies of progress. Two of these ideologies — which have suffered equally at the hands of crisis and disillusionment — have elements in common: the ideology of historical materialism, which sought to build a better world by means of revolution, and, of more concern to us here, the ideology of positivism and technology, which held that a better world could be built with science.

The Hidden Years. The 'modern' conception, wherein time passes in a cumulative and definable manner, stands in opposition to the Graeco-Roman tradition, in which time was conceived of as static

or cyclical; it replaced the fatalism of the ancients, which derived from the notion of subjection to an implacable nemesis. Humanity these days does not accord history a mystical dimension; as long as we are not living through periods of darkness and disillusionment, we tend to maintain our belief in the vectorial advance of time. Nowadays, people see the past as being known but not modifiable, and the future as being modifiable but unknown. Our general lack of certainty about what life has in store for us is assuaged not only by science fiction, but also by new projects for society, by reforms, by myths. However, we now know that time can no longer be understood in terms of a simplistic linear dynamic. More particularly, it cannot be understood within a perspective that is exclusively ascendant and that derives from the positivist, growth-oriented notions of the techno-industrial era.

There are various ways of speaking of the future,[1] of understanding it and of predicting a reality that is hidden from us and not easily susceptible of discovery: people set about attempting to divine, to read signs, to describe, to conjecture, to imagine and to dream what has yet to come into being. And each of

these activities has its own separate discipline: divination, prophecy, futurology, science fiction and utopias.

For a long time, to speak of or to reveal the future was seen as a dangerous, taboo act which belonged to the realm of magic, religion and the sacred. Soothsayers, shamans, druids, oracles, prophets, priests and sorcerers were the only ones with the power to see into that forbidden territory, and to reveal to those who came for advice the part which it was felt proper to reveal. Simple man eagerly devoured the chimeras, prognostications and prodigies that he was offered, and was thankful for meanings which could give an orientation to his life, his destiny and his place on earth. The view that life in heaven would be better than life on earth tended to push to one side the search for a decent life before death.

With the emergence of science, the irrational tended to go into decline. The present became clearer, while the future became permitted territory. It then became easier to imagine — to magnify the general tendencies which appeared to constitute history, and to project them forward: in short, to conjecture. If we are seeking the

3. *Cyrano de Bergerac flies off towards the sun. 1662*

The Travellers. Of all the species living on the earth, only *homo sapiens* knows what tomorrow is going to mean. Ever since the days when he portrayed himself in rock paintings as the hunter standing, victorious, over the animal he was going to kill, he has projected his own image before him, and has transported himself varying distances forward into a time that lies ahead of the present moment of indecision, a time where things are already a *fait accompli*.

In the realm of fiction there are few stories in antiquity which can really be said to describe future worlds. What we have instead is people travelling in strange countries, where they might meet inhuman creatures and fabulous hybrid beings, sometimes without heads and with curious attributes. The history of literature is full of 'adventures': Homer's *Odyssey*; the *Voyage to the Moon* of Lucian of Antioch (*c*. AD 160); Ariosto's *Orlando Furioso* (1516); Francis Godwin's *The Man in the Moone* (1638); Cyrano de Bergerac's *Histoire comique des états et empires de la Lune* (1657), followed by his *Histoire comique des états et royaumes du Soleil* (1662). All these were responding to the thirst for knowledge raised by the

existence of the unknown, and to the need to fill in the areas of virgin territory on the maps — those legendary *terræ incognitæ*, the zones beyond which, people said, the known world came to an end and the seas plunged into a bottomless abyss. A similar curiosity was aroused by the sight of the stars as they hung in the bowl of the night sky, moving with the rhythm of the days and months. Pre-scientific man was able to satisfy his curiosity about those parts of the world that were still foreign and unexplored through stories and travellers' tales that were packed with marvels and supernatural happenings. His voyage of discovery by proxy was not over-troubled by a concern for practical detail.

Later texts were to adopt a more satirical or philosophical approach. Thus Swift has his hero Gulliver travel to Lilliput, the country of the small people; to Brobdignag, the land of giants; to the land of scientists and their flying island of Laputa; and then to the country of the Houyhnhnms, a breed of intelligent horses which ruled over uncouth and uncivilised humans. Similar themes were explored by other writers who set out to prefigure the future, but at the time when *Gulliver's Travels* was published (1726) projection through time was less important than fictional geographical travels which offered opportunities for transposing references from the here and now, and enabled the writer to establish the distance necessary for satire to be effective and for imparting the requisite element of mystery to the story. The parts of the world then being explored had not yet been mapped, and much remained to be discovered. As time went by, people increasingly felt that the world was a small place, and that soon it would no longer be large enough to satisfy human appetites. Voltaire understood this, and sent, in *Micromégas*, his eponymous hero down to earth (1752). This giant inhabitant of Sirius travels down through space and lands on earth, whereupon he contrives to hold philosophical conversations with 'invisible insects' — in other words, human beings.

roots of the myth of the year 2000, we find them in the field Pierre Versins has called 'rational fictional conjecture', which originated in this period.[2] It excludes fantasy, parapsychology and the supernatural. The 'futures' of astrologers and magicians, the speculations of mystics, the predictions of millenarists and other prophetic visionaries do not concern themselves with a description of the future in terms that are palpable and pseudo-realist. But the field also excludes works in futurology, which, inversely, are inclined to follow the laws of big numbers and of probability, and end by overstating the effects of statistical demonstration.

The writers and illustrators of the industrial era, whose aim was to entertain and sometimes to question, have left us a record of their voyages into the future, voyages which enabled their readers to imagine, describe and depict events that were going to happen sooner or later — tomorrow or in the year 2000; in their world or in other worlds; in a future which could sometimes be radiant and wonderful, but which could equally be fearsome to behold.

4. *Flying 1,000 kilometres non-stop. 1889*

The Age of Revolution. The philosophy of the Enlightenment was a frontal assault on the bastions of superstition, obscurantism and religion. It was to prepare the ground for science, technology and industry, in that it favoured a vision of the world that was based on the first two, and thereby enabled the emergence of the third. The eighteenth century put a premium on knowledge, rationality and faith in progress. In 1729, the Englishman Ephraim Chambers attempted a first compilation of human knowledge, in his *Cyclopaedia*, or *Dictionary of Arts and Sciences*. But the *Encyclopédie ou Dictionnaire raisonné des sciences, des arts et des métiers pour une societé de gens de lettres* — the encyclopaedia prepared by Diderot and d'Alembert in 1751-72 — stands as the most remarkable example of the new organisation of knowledge that was being pursued by philosophers, within which science occupied a pride of place which it had snatched from theology. The world was no longer a dark realm of mystery and anxiety. Everything had to be susceptible of explanation, analysis and demonstration.

By the start of the twentieth century, the march of progress — persuasive, radiant and ineluctable — was to cut broad swathes through towns and villages alike, as well as through the habits and mentalities of people. The transition from human and animal labour to mechanisation signalled the birth of the Industrial Revolution, which originated in Britain at the end of the eighteenth century. Once tamed, the new sources of energy enabled industrialisation to introduce a range

of new concepts, such as the workforce and efficiency. Rational explanations for worldly phenomena were able to satisfy the curiosity sparked by the appearance — at the level of everyday life too — of new technologies. 'The scientist conceives something, the technician invents it, the industrialist makes it, universal expositions advertise it to a public, big department stores make it available, the press creates an expectation, provokes new desires, and above all gives the consumer the certainty that progress is a precondition of happiness.'[3] These were the days when the future was regarded as foreseeable, qualitatively superior, unidirectional, and susceptible to human control.[4]

In 1851, London saw the opening of the Great Exhibition, in the Crystal Palace that had been designed and built by Joseph Paxton. Cities were being rationalised, adapting themselves to the transformations taking place in the means of production, consumption and transportation. Printed matter, especially in the form of newspapers, achieved extraordinary print runs. The penny broadsheet and the *petit journal* came into being to satisfy the needs of a readership that was impatient for novelty; when they became

5. *Jules Verne creates a new literary genre: the science fiction novel.*

6. *Travelators at the Exposition Universelle offered visitors a foretaste of locomotion in the future. 1900*

'illustrated', their readers' interest redoubled. The world was a mechanical and everyday thing, but it was also extraordinary and full of adventure — and it belonged to them. They moved from being readers to becoming users of progress. Education, which was increasingly seen as having a democratic function, served to pass on this growing body of knowledge. The process was helped by the existence of reading matter which saw itself as being educational as well as recreational, for example, the *Magasin d'éducation et de récréation* published by Pierre-Jules Hetzel in 1862. In the same period, a twenty-year-old astronomer by the name of Camille Flammarion published his first work, *La Pluralité des mondes habités*. His talents as a populariser did a lot to interest a broader public in the topic of astronomy and the realm of the future.

The Scientific Novel. This was the context in which Jules Verne (1828-1905) made his appearance. Reflecting perfectly the spirit of the times, he was the first to achieve a synthesis of adventure-filled fiction with rational scientific detail. A new genre was born: the scientific novel. Verne

succeeded in reconciling imagination and reason, showing that a rigorous scientific approach could perfectly well provide the substance of a novel. With only rare exceptions — *Amiens en l'an 2000*; *La journée d'un journaliste américain en 2889*; *L'éternel Adam* — his texts were located not in the future, but in a present situated in a near future; they consisted of extrapolations from knowledge available at the time and Verne never transgressed the bounds of that knowledge; his most daring devices — the giant cannons, Captain Nemo's submarine, Robur's dirigible — were direct descendants of the huge artillery pieces of the American Civil War, of the first submarines which were just coming into service at that time, and of the helicopters of Ponton d'Amécourt and La Landelle. Verne was insistent on the verisimilitude of the things that he portrayed; he expected the technical detail to match the seriousness of his conjectures. Retrospectively we can admire the accuracy of his hypotheses: for example, that it was fired from Florida, and that the speed of the rocket was almost exactly that of the jettisoning of the third stage of Apollo IX in July 1969. However, we cite Verne more for his general historical importance in the field, since he does not strictly fall within the terms of reference of our book — namely, projections into the future.

Still in France, Albert Robida proved to be perhaps the most enjoyable antidote to Jules Verne's rationality. In 1879 he published an undisguised satire on Verne: *Voyages très extraordinaires de Saturnin Farandoul dans les cinq ou six parties du monde et dans tous les pays connus et même inconnus de M. Jules Verne*. Robida was an illustrator, a caricaturist and a prolific author. He illustrated his own texts, and his work reflected a powerful imagination, and a subtle vision that combined with a fantastical and satirical view of the future. His contributions to the fictional history of the future were principally *La Guerre au xxᵉ siècle* (1883), *Le Vingtième siècle* (1883) and *La Vie électrique* (1893), as well as the illustrations for *La Guerre infernale* by Pierre Giffard (1908) and for a number of magazines, in particular *La Caricature*, of which he was editor. Robida avoids didacticism, and with wit and an occasional acute sense of prophecy he succeeds in painting a vision of the future which is sometimes attractive, but more often sinister. His work is constantly informed with philosophical humour, and he is sufficiently detached not to allow his imagination to get bogged down in short-term prediction.

Thinking of the Future. Herbert George Wells (1866-1946) was another key exponent of the art of anticipational writing. He is often compared and contrasted with Jules Verne, and certainly benefited from the favourable climate created by the latter's work. However, he starts out from a different viewpoint. In contrast to the punctilious rationality of Verne, Wells has a tendency to allusive prediction and philosophy. Where Verne took a keen delight in describing machines, calculations, technology and the details of journeys, Wells tended to tread the path of speculation, applying himself to a description of the effects of newly emerging knowledge on the human spirit, and to advancing a system of ideas. He published his first science fiction story — *The Time Machine* — in 1895. This was followed by *A History of Future Time* (1897), *When the Sleeper Awakes* (1899), which is set in the twenty-second century, and then his *A Modern Utopia* (1905). He had no illusions about the benefits of progress, but steered clear of pessimism. He was more daring in his novels than in his formal futurological studies, which tended to be serious and moralistic. Wells had a voluntarist attitude

7. *Portable aerials would make it possible for people to receive declarations of love or the racing results by wireless telegraphy. 1906*

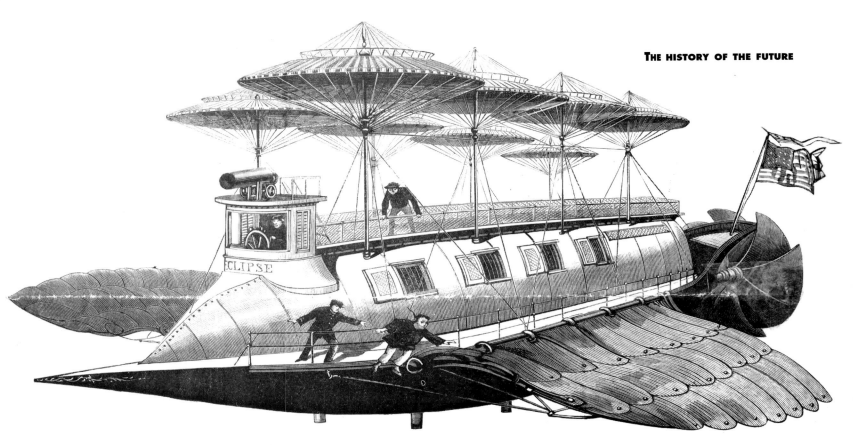

8. *In the 19th century, 'dime novels' popularised scientific discoveries in a technological mishmash of stories for young people. 1892*

towards the future: 'I believe that it would be extremely stimulating and profitable for our intellectual life to direct historical, economic and social studies towards the future, and in religious and moral debates to concern ourselves more with the future, to address it constantly, deliberately and courageously.'[5]

A Popular Current. In the wake of Verne and Wells, we find a number of writers tapping into this vein of tales of voyages and extraordinary adventures, where the scientific detail is supplied by the recent discoveries in science: electricity, telephones, wireless telegraphy, submarines and various sorts of aircraft. In France the genre experienced a boost in the writings of a generation of authors such as Maurice Renard (*Le Péril bleu*, 1910; *L'Homme truqué*, 1921); G. Le Faure and H. de Graffigny (*Les Aventures extraordinaires d'un savant russe*, 1889-96); J.-H. Rosny Sr (*La Mort de la Terre*, 1910); and Anatole France (*L'Île des pingouins*, 1908). In the Anglo-Saxon world, we find Sir Arthur Conan Doyle (*The Poisoned Belt*, 1913), George Griffith (*Olga Romanov*, 1897), Jack London (*The Iron Heel*, 1907; *The Scarlet Plague*, 1912) and Rudyard Kipling (*With the Night Mail*, 1905).

In the dissemination of the future as a literary genre, an indispensable role was played by general literary and popularising magazines — 'scientific recreation', as it was called at the time. Thus we had *Lectures pour tous*, *Je sais tout* and *Sciences et voyages*, illustrated by

Albert Robida and Henri Lanos. In Britain, science fiction stories and articles popularising science appeared in *Cassell's Magazine*, *Pearson's Magazine*, *The Strand* and various boys' magazines of the period. Illustrators of the time included Paul Hardy, Warwick Goble and Fred T. Jane. The genre experienced a similar wave of popularisation in other European countries; in Germany, for instance, Robert Kraft plagiarised fashionable ideas, and Robert Heymann published a serialised work, called the *Wunder der Zukunft*, a sequence of novels exploring the third millennium.

In the United States, a mass literature was available in the form of small magazines printed on cheap paper. These 'dime novels' also existed in a cheaper version — the 'half-dime' novel — and were sold for a dime or a nickel a piece. They were the equivalent of the novels sold for two or four sous on French railway stations at the time. All kinds of subjects were tackled, but science fiction made its entry in 1868, with the appearance of the Steam Man, a robot employed in tracking down Indians (Edward S. Ellis, *The Steam Man of the Prairies*). A second edition was published in 1876, which enjoyed such success that the publisher commissioned more of the same from other writers. This led to the appearance of the inventor Frank Reade, and his robot The Steam Man of the Plains. Luis Philip Senarens, a prolific writer in a variety of fields, took up the idea and developed it further, transforming the hero into a young man by the name of Frank

Reade Jr, and entertaining his readers with a series of publications signed with the *nom de plume* Noname. Inspired by Jules Verne, he wrote adventure stories against a technological and scientific backdrop. He described a future world that was full of improbable and poetic inventions, featuring air and land vehicles, rockets, helicopters and submarines.

The end of the nineteenth century saw a variety of other popular magazines printed on cheap papers. Crudely produced on pulp paper, these paperbacks with their limp, yellowing pages and their brightly coloured illustrated covers were known as 'pulps', and the name stuck with them over the years. The oldest of them was the magazine *Argosy*. Edgar Rice Burroughs, the creator of Tarzan, wrote the Martian adventures of one John Carter in the magazine *Allstory*. Elsewhere, Hugo Gernsback, a Luxembourger who became a naturalised American, was branching out into electronics, and published a number of technical magazines devoted to electricity, radio and engineering: *Modern Electrics*, *Electrical Experimenter* and *Science and Invention*. In one edition of *Modern Electrics* he printed a science fiction story that teemed with 'prophetic' details: *Ralph 124 C 41+*. In Britain, as in France, the reading public was developing a passionate interest in motor vehicles and flying machines of all kinds, and had its curiosity aroused by magazine articles which revealed, for example, the secrets of radio communication with the planet Mars.

Amazing Stories. Then the future crossed the Atlantic, and an American view of things tended to take over. In 1926, Hugo Gernsback launched the first science fiction magazine, *Amazing Stories*, and at the same time invented the term 'scientifiction', which in 1929 became 'science fiction'. This was the first magazine in a series with a long and lively history, which has been thoroughly studied in the books of Jacques Sadoul, Anthony Frewin, David Kyle and Brian Aldiss. The rupture caused by the First World War meant that European writers could no longer fantasize with the innocence typical of the previous century; they slipped instead into pessimism and disillusionment, or the recycling of tired clichés. Gernsback had initiated a mechanical, experimental 'technophile' trend in the United States, which was ably evoked in graphic terms by the artist Frank R. Paul. It now became possible to illustrate the genre in a different, more popular fashion, exploring visually all the themes that authors were exploring in their writing. Very early on, Gernsback was publishing H. G. Wells's stories in his magazines, and in 1929 he launched *Wonder Stories*. A competing publication, *Astounding Stories*, was launched in 1930, under the edit-orship of Harry Bates. It was of rather better quality than most of the other pulps, and continued to maintain a certain pre-eminence, with authors such as Ray Cummings, David H. Keller, Abraham Merritt, and the illustrators H. M. Wesso and Elliot Dold.

Alongside Gernsback, another key figure in the evolution of science fiction was John W. Campbell Jr, a writer and science enthusiast who took over the editorship of *Astounding Stories* in 1937. He played a prime role as editor of the magazine, encouraging his authors and helping the genre to escape from the childish routines in which it was initially mired. The authors whom he published included Isaac Asimov, Alfred E. van Vogt, Robert Heinlein and Lewis Padgett. Science fiction 'pulps' enjoyed a considerable success right up to the early 1940s, with large print runs and a wide range of titles. They included *Planet Stories*, *Startling Stories*, *Fantastic Adventures*, *Super Science Fiction*, and in addition, for an even wider audience, comic strips featuring the likes of Buck Rogers, Brick Bradford, Flash Gordon, and Superman.

We can trace a certain evolution in these stories. The naïvety of early ventures in the field is soon left behind. In 1905, following the work of Max Planck in quantum physics, Albert Einstein's theory of relativity broke with Newtonian mechanics. Subsequently, the abandonment of the idea of a universal ether and the new physical properties implied by this radical change in the concept of the universe made gradual headway both in the scientific world and among the new wave of science fiction writers. The genre was in its Golden Age, and put the notion of relativity to good use, plumbing the paradoxical nature of the theory in order to enrich new forms of conjecture regarding the nature of time and space. At the same time one notes a decrease in euphoria, the establishment of a critical distance in relation to science, and, following the Great Depression and the Second World War, a rejection of grand ideas about the future.

Put schematically, science fiction writing began from a technological and ethnocentric base in 1850, and by the start of the 1960s it had succeeded in exploring and categorising the future in ways that were both convincing and comprehensive. Throughout this period, writers ventured into a more or less pagan future for humanity, and brought back kaleidoscopic and bustling visions that Alfred Jarry would have loved — lightning flashes of truth in the social, sexual, psychic and technological domains, within space and within the infinity of time.

9. *Obscure inventors tried their hand at building — often badly — the world of the future. 1901*

Prediction in the Hands of Humorists. Projection into the future is such a temptation for humorists that it can become a formula. It is easy to make one's contemporaries laugh by transposing to a few years ahead the follies of bicycle mania or the spread of air transport, or a world turned upside down, with, say, women taking over. The future is a godsend for popular humorists, for comic illustrators, for strip cartoonists, for political caricaturists, and for animators such as Tex Avery, who has given us four different projections into tomorrow's world. A delightful example of parody appeared in the six issues of *L'Autre monde, journal des trépassées*, which was printed on black paper in 1877, carrying a by-line for the year 3753. This was a satirical political newspaper which had a good time stringing together unlikely events and spoofing advertisements.

In Jean-Ignace Isidore Gérard, known as Grandville, we have a rare and extravagant creator of — to use his own words — gracious monstrosities, thanks to his ability to let his imagination float free. He was a surveyor of

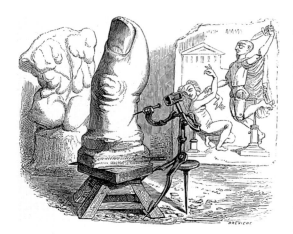

10. *A far-fetched voyage in Another World. 1844*

the unconscious, a precursor of the surrealists, and his pen transposed onto paper large-scale puns and visual puzzles that gave a plastic form to dreams and nightmares. According to Baudelaire, Grandville did this with the precision of a shorthand note-taker copying down a speech. In 1844, his fantastical imagery, based on dream visions and associations of ideas, was used to illustrate *Un autre monde*.

A number of his plates were to be reprinted in the third part of *Le Diable à Paris*, entitled 'Paris Futur'. With Grandville one becomes aware of the distance that separates rational anticipation from fantastical invention. What guides Grandville is the same thing that moves Edgar Allan Poe, Odilon Redon, H. P. Lovecraft and the Maupassant of *Horla*: namely, dreams, the unconscious, and buried visions which take shape in the creator's mind and are then unleashed and allowed to reach the conscious level, where they are given form by means of writing or drawing.

The collages of Max Ernst, in particular some of the images from *La Femme 100 têtes* (1929), have an affinity with some of our more apocalyptic visions of the future. The unexpected bursts forth from a contrapuntal arrangement of 'dry' images which are taken out of context and juxtaposed, so that their very banality imparts a sense of strangeness: the pieces have titles which use a grammatical future tense in order to announce coming events that are both prophetic and oneiric. Disasters and upheavals are not avoided but announced and awaited, as welcome as the morning dew. In Ernst, as in other Dadaists and surrealists, one notes an undisguised fascination with elaborate mechanical constructions which are useless but at the same time all-powerful, combining poetry and machinery in a marriage that is both contrary to nature and disturbing.

The Closed World of the Utopias. In science fiction, projection into the future takes place through the imagination. In Utopian fiction, people are transported to a fictional place unfamiliar to humanity. The geographical location is unspecified — a 'Utopia', from the Greek *ou topos*, meaning nonplace, nowhere. The first Utopia was that created in the well-known social and political novel of that name written in England by Sir Thomas More (1516). Having painted a highly critical picture of the Europe of his period, he advanced an idealised vision of a society in which his proposed solutions were already in operation; but he situated this society on an undiscovered island. More was followed by other authors, like Tommaso Campanella (*La Città del sole*, 1623) and Francis Bacon (*The New Atlantis*, 1626). Many other literary Utopists were to embark on fictional writing about cities that were beyond the pale of the real, the creations of societies that were ideal, philosophical and rationally governed.

Within the closed world of these Utopias, time does not exist, so the future is of no concern. Nevertheless, for some authors this 'nowhere' corresponds in fictional terms to a future, and it is within this framework that

they describe the external appearance, the political organisation, the inhabitants and the lifestyle of the place in question. There, the advance of civilisation and the development of human understanding are portrayed as having taken a far faster route, and the comparison between these Utopian societies and that of the writer gives the image of a world situated in the future, ahead of the writer's own. This may be the case,[6] for example, in the above-mentioned texts by Cyrano de Bergerac and in the writings of Nicolas-Edme Restif de la Bretonne, in *La Découverte australe par un homme volant le Dédale français* (1781). This 'acceleration of history' forms the basis for the Atlantis myth, created by Plato, which has recently given rise to a number of variants.

Louis-Sébastian Mercier, with his *L'An 2440, ou Rêve s'il en fut jamais* (1770), was the first to advance beyond nostalgia for the Golden Age by situating the happy society he describes in a future time. The Utopian current is fundamental to the eighteenth century. Projects for ideal societies were often described in clinical detail. But these Utopian cities were closed places, shut in on themselves, functioning

11. *Max Ernst's surrealist collages gave rise to terrifying poems and prophetic dreams. 1929*

in a repetitive mode within cosmic time. This excludes them from history and *a fortiori* from the future, since the only meaning of time is as its own eternal rebeginning, blocking notions of progress and improvement. Caprice and chance are anathema — they are banned from the confines of the rational and immutable city.[7]

The nineteenth century saw the development of a Utopian current which inclined to reformism and the perfection of an ordered society based on socialist ideas. This current inspired a number of written texts. One thinks of Claude Henri de Saint-Simon and

the devotees of Saint-Simonism, but also Charles Fourier (*L'Harmonie universelle* and *Le Phalanstère*, 1849), Robert Owen (*A New View of Society, or essays on the principle of the formation of the human character*, 1813) and Etienne Cabet (*Voyage en Icarie*, 1840). Fourier's phalanstery was to be realised in real life — in Godin's Familistère at Guise in the Aisne region, and in a number of colonies set up in America by followers of Owen, Fourier and Cabet; these were the only instances to be tested against reality.

One also finds a number of fictional Utopias which are projections into the future: Edward Bellamy's *Looking Backward* (1887), and William Morris's *News from Nowhere* (1891). There were already counterposing tendencies in some of the Utopias portrayed, but during the period covered in this volume a split occurred between a happy Utopia — sometimes called Eutopia — and an evil Utopia, or anti-Utopia — Dystopia, counter-Utopia — which represents a pessimistic rad-icalisation of the notion of Utopia and of the murderous tendencies of the societies it seeks to describe and denounce. Thus, following in the footsteps of Swift, we have Samuel Butler's *Erewhon* (an anagram of 'nowhere', 1872), but more particularly a number of twentieth-

century authors who set out to denounce the horrors of totalitarianism: Yevgeny Zamyatin (*We*, 1920), Aldous Huxley (*Brave New World*, 1932) and George Orwell (*1984*, 1949). These fearsome anti-Utopian societies are framed in a future which is more or less round the corner, and can be both prophetic and alarming.

Kaleidoscope. In the various visions of the future that we have mentioned, the role of images is both symbolic and rational, but more intuitive than logical. We have fantastical drawings, many inspired by humour, poetry or allegory, often playing an emblematic role: Robida's *Le Déblaiement du vieux monde* springs to mind, as does Jack London's *The Scarlet Plague*, illustrated by Gordon Grant. However, a majority of the illustrations are 'realistic' images because they have an illustrative, demonstrative, explicative or documentary function. These 'real' illustrations attempt to give a clear, detailed, plausible, but anecdotal vision of a scene. They often appear as covers, or as illustrations within the texts. The 'demonstrative' images come as part of a series, and express process and evolution; they exist only as a function of an accumulation, of a logical sequence, or of a mutual relationship: here we may include advertising images and cartoon strips. The 'explanatory' images, on the other hand, imitate scientific drawings, offering cross-sections, plans and blow-ups, and they tend to be carefully annotated; the most striking examples come from the back covers of the pulp magazines. The 'documentary' images are extremely precise drawings, or faked photographs,

12. *Above: Car manufacturers always bill their prototypes as 'the car of tomorrow'. 1965*

13. *Left: Even before the First World War was declared, it was possible to sense the dominant role that technology would play in it. 1910*

14. *Below: Chaplin poked fun at the absurdity of progress, its shortcomings and its failures. 1936*

15. *Right: Grandville imagined a crazy steam concert. 1844*

LE MOI
ET LE
NON MOI
SYMPHONIE
EN UT
MAJEUR

playing the journalistic role of a press photograph. Film, by its nature, falls into this latter category, but its symbolic content may be very powerful (*Metropolis*, *Forbidden Planet*).

These images belong to a world of illusion; they are, however, the route by which we attempt to pierce the fog from which will emerge the prefigurations of the future. Some of these illustrations are so concrete, so teeming with detail, and seem marked with such a strong internal coherence that one envies the imagination responsible, or one is, on the contrary, relieved not to have such a sharp, vivid imagination. Here we should cite the illustrations of Frank R. Paul, Henri Lanos, Elliott Dold, Leo Morey and Ed Emshwiller, known as Emsh. Their images are so realistic as to become creators and founders of an imaginary future world, reinforcing the texts that brought them into being. Their sheer power infuses them with a feeling of independent existence, as if they had been activated by their own mode of narration and by the futurist mythology of their visual discourse.

These visions — drawn, engraved, painted, or on film — are organised in the collective unconscious as a set of archetypal forms: machines which seem to come out of some giant Meccano set; rockets; flying saucers; astronauts; little green men; android robots and gigantic cities.

16. *A complicated machine for eating peas.*

The Game of Conjecture. One of humanity's greatest dreams is to be able to probe the mists of the future, which appear to us as impenetrable as space itself. Once all the blank areas on geographical maps had been filled, the new frontier became a temporal one. The nineteenth and twentieth centuries were able to reconcile imagination with a taste for mechanical engineering, and their imagination peopled radiant tomorrows with robot slaves, with automated houses and rationally ordered societies. And all this could be made visible with a stroke of the pen, or the turn of a magazine page. The extrapolations follow the foreseeable progress of history, but are not necessarily able to take on board the acceleration brought about by major new discoveries and sudden advances in technology. The temporal paradox of the extrapolator is the fact that his is a static voyage within time; when he embarks on his voyage he takes with him the mentality, the understanding and the discoveries characteristic of his own era.

There is also a temporal tie-up in another form — not grammatical, but sociological: one has the future of one's own present; more particularly, the future that one imagines is inevitably inscribed within a viewpoint limited by the myopia of the present. The writer of imaginary scientific fiction is using material already rendered out of date by popularisation. To say 'in a hundred years' time' a hundred years ago was never more than to conjugate into the future the technology, the ideas of justice, the desires for freedom and well-being of the writer's present time: the way of life is identical, simply transposed. Each epoch has produced its own year 2000, as a metaphorical image of life, but can we nowadays accept these new Cassandras holding up their deforming mirrors and proclaiming the 'unlivability' of the future? The spectrum of views of the future ranges from the pessimistic to the optimistic.

Behind conjecture lies a concern to re-orientate the future by means of the projection one makes of it, and to shape it by means of a negative image — in the photographic sense — or by a virtual image, which will (or will not) come into existence and reveal itself under the combined action of a chemistry of light and time. By this we mean that it passes through a chronological developing bath, and a contemporaneous fixing solution, which is what gives this image its reality — its good parts (clear-edged projection), its defects (over- or under-exposure) and its poetry (soft focus, montage effects,

17. *The lyrical form of the* Monument to the Third International. *1919*

touching up). The photo of the future is always doctored, constantly affirming both its lack of realism and a preoccupation with giving a sense of time.

Back into the mists which precede universal, historical, Western time (the time that can be represented symbolically by an arrow), another time stretches, in monstrous multiple outline. This is the time of the future — multiform, uncontained and diffuse — time as it was before it became linear and univocal. It sometimes turns into an exercise in style which becomes intoxicated with its possibilities, for no potential future projection may be rejected *a priori*. Space has to be made for the intervention of pure fantasy, paying out its metaphors in the way that electricity is strung out from one tower block to another in Robida — exaggeration for the pleasure of creating unexpected effects, or simply by way of amusement. Future time is spread out like a luminous mosaic; many of the lights will go out with the passing of the given historical moment, leaving behind only the outline. Projection into the future is not subject to the sanctions of either reality or censorship: the future offers itself as virgin, and not as *fait accompli*. Dream is the light which exposes these plates; the passing of time will develop some of them, or at least some of their details, while leaving others in the props cupboard of an imagination that has been overtaken by events in real life.

A Panorama of the Future. In the plurality of hypotheses on offer, one can distinguish varying degrees: from the chanciest of conjectures to the probability of accomplishment, from dubious predictions to the fortuitous accident, from the virtual to the *fait accompli*, from the inevitable to the impossible. To prejudge the future is to risk repudiation or sarcasm at the hands of posterity, or to win posthumous admiration for a debatable correctness of vision. It also happens that future centuries forget the people who had so correctly imagined them.

It is entirely possible that the world is a more beautiful place when it exists only as a vision. It is indeed risky to suppose a continuity, but in the business of conjecture one has to make the effort, while all the time attempting to foresee discontinuity. However, it is more important to put on a good display of imagination or intuition than to be precisely right in one's predictions. The further forward an artist projects his thought, the more inventive his ideas are. Only temporal distance enables him to free himself from the present, from the reasonable, and to give his imagination full rein, unconstrained, like a child playing at make-believe. With a whole century before him (*a fortiori* if the distance is even greater), when a writer applies all his intellect, all his thought to describing a future which he will never know and which he has decided to situate a long way forward from his own present, he can permit himself to be inventive, hare-brained, naïve, detached, even irresponsible. He will not be there to see the future for himself, and he runs no risk of being contradicted or ridiculed in his own lifetime.

Some writers, in imagining the future, come across as too timid; others are too peremptory in their approach and appear to have problems in getting the measure of their subject; lacking a suitable yardstick, they may over- or underestimate likely trends. One may speak of a futurism that is 'life-size' and another that is 'magnifying'.[8] In the former, the projection is sufficiently precise for *a posteriori* verification to point to the realism and reasonableness of the way in which the future is portrayed. Some accounts are excessively modest, for reasons of caution or conformity. The 'magnifying' futurism, on the other hand, is characterised by a wildness of vision and deliberate exaggeration. The choice of contents for the future (progress or regression) and a desire to prove something may explain the presence of forced effects in the projection. There are also misjudgements about the rate of progress of science and technology, which is often faster than the accompanying psychological and moral evolution of society. Science fiction writers are often cited for their role as 'instigators', as 'whistle-blowers' warning of things to come. It is no accident that Jules Verne and the German Kurt Lasswitz are said to have had an influence on Einstein and on space industry pioneers such as Tsiolkovsky, Goddard and von Braun.c b,vv,

Fictional Chronologies. André Clément-Decouflé suggests that there are four kinds of dating in futuristic writing: intentional, reflex, conventional and arbitrary.[9] 'Intentional' dating, which is fairly rare, relates to a subjective certainty which is expressed in the choice of a date which has personal meaning for the author himself. This is the case with Ray Bradbury's *Martian Chronicles*, which begin in 1999, the year he imagines as the date of his own death. 'Reflex' dating reflects symbolic moments within a given socio-cultural tradition — for example round-figure millennia such as the year 2000, or the anniversaries of major historical events such as the American Revolution. Mankind has a certain fascination with the periodical turning-points offered by the calendar. Our imminent arrival at the third millennium raises longstanding questions: 'Our origins, the meaning of lost history, destiny rediscovered, eternity, an "end of time" which can once again be exorcised and put back for another thousand years — until the point when the drama of the year 3000 begins to be felt on the horizons of world history.'[10] 'Conventional' dating is established by common usage; it may, for example, refer to a particular date in the popular tradition, such as 1984, following the success of Orwell's novel. With 'arbitrary' dating, the action takes place after a gap of a round number of years or centuries: e.g. fifty or a thousand years in the future. With this formula, the most common form of arbitrary dating consists of setting the action in the same year the book was written, but in a different century. Thus in 1889 Jules Verne wrote and published in the United States a short story entitled *La Journée d'un journaliste américain en 2889*: its dating is arbitrary but not aleatory.

In this ritual of dating, which seems to be more or less mechanical and obligatory among the writers of futurist fiction, Decouflé sees a caricature of history carried to crazy extremes. If we were to examine science fiction writing and produce a chronology which respected the various arbitrary dates proposed by authors, we would find some ludicrous juxtapositions: a 'thousand-year' projection into the year 2900 showing vehicles travelling at the incredible speed of eighteen miles per hour and Montgolfier balloons as the universal means of transport[11] would follow on from the year 2300, when telepathic police and psychic analysts would be arresting criminals by penetrating into their brains,[12] and people would routinely travel in highly sophisticated means of transport. An objective fictional chronology could follow the course of the real dates of publication of the texts and could rectify their more excessive errors of projection, measuring each step in the progress of the future in the light of the achievements actually accomplished during the twentieth century, and in the light of foreseeable advances, of futurist extrapolations and of unexpected breakthroughs; this 'history of the future' would also have to be corrected in the light of the evolutionary curves of civilisations (birth, rise and fall).

However, many stories since 1851 address themselves only to the rising phase, marked by a triumphant technicity and a progress that follows an exponential growth curve. In *Memories of the Future*, John Atkins advances an entertaining reading, albeit over a fairly restricted period, of science fiction novels. These are treated as

18. *Karel Čapek launches the first robots with RUR: Rossum Universal Robots. 1921*

19. *The lunar module visualised by H. G. Wells in his novel* The First Men in the Moon, *which was adapted for the cinema. 1964*

primary sources, and his hero, an imaginary historian in the year 3750, finds in them all the material necessary for a detailed reconstruction of the events which preceded his own era (1960 to 3750), events of which the only remaining trace is a set of science fiction novels which he discovers preserved in a buried library.

Historical Reference Points. In order to grab the reader's attention, projections into the future have to provide human points of reference. These permit the traveller — the readers of time stories, of stories of discovery and exploration — to make comparisons and to get their bearings, enabling them to locate the projected future, however distant it may be, within a historical continuum. Otherwise it remains closed on itself, and would function in a void. Sometimes the author may use references that are recognisable but slightly altered, as in fiction based on real people. However diluted, however masked, the human model can still be identified.

Within this exercise of projection into the future, there is also an attempt at 'distancing', at providing a different viewpoint.

Just as Montesquieu, in his *Persian Letters*, presented a view of Western society as seen by two visitors from the Middle East, the science fiction writer provides a definition of humanity, of cities and of war as seen through the eyes of a stranger who may be a man living a thousand years in the future, or, more likely, an extraterrestrial, a robot, or even a dog. Clifford D. Simak, for example created a canine historian who related a series of legendary tales inherited from human civilisation; he gives brief definitions of a number of concepts unfamiliar to his peers: 'Killing is a process, usually involving violence by which one living thing ends the life of another living thing. War, it would appear, was mass killing carried out on a scale which is inconceivable.'[13]

A Science Fiction Emporium. The body of works that we discuss are drawn from a hundred-year period, from 1851 to 1961. Since a new century is not necessarily born in year one, but perhaps ten or fifteen years before or after, the date for the earliest material in our collection has no need to be fixed arbitrarily at a symbolic

20. *Boullée, the visionary architect, proposed Utopian monuments that future generations would neglect. 1784*

year of round figures. One might have thought of setting it as far back as 1837, with Queen Victoria's accession to the throne, or 1840, with the first photograph of the moon, or 1848, the year of revolution in Europe, or 1863, when the first of Jules Verne's *Voyages extraordinaires* was published. The year 1851, however, provides an acceptable milestone — the Great Exhibition in London. This event was designed to exhibit important new inventions and products.

The choice of a suitable year for an end-point is less easy and inevitably more arbitrary, since there is really no reason for not including writings right up to the present day. There is, however, an identifiable historical divide that splits the twentieth century irrevocably into a 'before' and an 'after', and marks the end of a dream: this was 1961, with the first launching of a man into space. Around this date we find a cluster of other dates that strengthen its importance: 1953, when the structure of DNA was discovered, marking the beginning of molecular biology and neurophysiology; 1957, the launching of Sputnik I, the earth's first artificial satellite; 1960, the appearance of the laser (light amplification by stimulated emission of radiation); 1962, the Cuban crisis and the high point of the Cold War; 1965, large-scale US intervention in Vietnam. By 1960 we are already on the road to cybernetics and miniaturisation; humanity was soon to become aware of the dangers inherent in a civilisation founded on machinery. After Yuri Gagarin's journey into space in 1961, the decade is punctuated by significant dates, right up until 21 July 1969, when Neil Armstrong and Edwin Aldrin walk on the moon. After 1960, the year 2000 dies as a dream. It has been demystified; reality has replaced the imaginary. The future is now set on a path of the probable, and no longer the possible. Transparent domes over cities are no longer viable. We suspected as much anyway. In the event, the subject of our dreams — the year 2000 — is arriving quickly.

And as the real year 2000 comes closer, the available gap becomes too short, and the forecasts too true, too concrete and effective. Anyway, by 1961, the majority of authors were losing interest in it, and were beginning to project their fictions further forward in time, since, between them and the fictional year we have chosen as the subject of this book, there remained only another four decades or so.

21. *The Cité Industrielle by Tony Garnier was ahead of its time and advocated the zoning of activities. 1917*

Temporal Filters. We have chosen to take in only science fiction in its literary form, leaving aside both actual scientific texts and those that enter the realm of the irrational. The principal criterion, however, is temporality: we have chosen anticipatory works in the proper sense of the term, that is to say, writings and graphics dated in the future, however vague or specific that future. While the future tense is often employed in articles popularising points of interest in science, it is seldom used in science fiction stories. The narrator generally places himself centuries or millennia ahead in the future, in the demiurgic, all-powerful position of a storyteller or a historian giving an account of past events.

The documents which are closest to projections into the future come from science fiction stories where we have a fictional present with all the hallmarks of a future tense. Here the author tells of events that are going to happen — as we well know — such as the landing on the moon, or the conquest of the ocean bed, as well as less likely occurences, such as descending into the bowels of the earth: here the reader will recognise Jules Verne, not to mention Georges Méliès and Hergé. However, these

'historic' moments are not seen as being in the future, or 'anticipated'. They take place in the present tense of the reader and of the author. In the wake of recent discoveries (aeroplanes, cars and rockets), all kinds of geographical, aerial and financial conquest are undertaken, and the stories describing them have a journalistic tone in which the events are covered in a more or less documentary spirit. These stories provide classic, enduring images which take their place in the collective unconscious, such as the cannon-fired space rocket, or green, tentacled Martians. Barbicane, Mabouloff and Tintin are real heroes, not beings from a future world telling a story. What we have here is an extension of the literature of geographic adventure and exoticism; jungles, far-off landscapes and cannibals are replaced by space, the moon, Mars, carnivorous plant-animals, and a variety of cruel and intelligent beings. The game is faked here, because, although they represent a future that has not yet happened, these texts have not entered into the game-play of distance. The prophesy has already been realised within the fiction, as it were, and thus the element of the future is absent.

Some of these writings portray (fictional) past civilisations as having reached a high level of technological perfection: here we have a kind of futurist past. As well as Atlantis, the lost continent of Mu, and various pre-Columbian and Pacific civilisations, we have stories that are situated in a past period, or in a place cut off from the real world (this may be an island, or an inaccessible valley), tracing the history of a highly advanced civilisation which is dramatically destroyed. In one of Alexei Tolstoy's novels, *Aelita* (1923), the people of Atlantis had fled their country after it had been engulfed twenty thousand years previously. An egg-shaped machine enabled them to reach Mars, and they took their scientific knowledge with them. In José Moselli's *La Fin d'Illa* (1925), flying saucers pulverise invisible enemies, there is a revolt of the monkey-men, human blood is the main source of energy, and an entire civilisation is wiped out by an all-destroying weapon.[14]

One Mile High. Architecture has an obvious relationship with the realm of the future. Here one finds as many implications, question marks and ideological statements as one is likely to find in other visions of the future, but all grounded in rationality, without the literary element of fiction. When they are 'visionary', the works of artists and architects enter fairly naturally — by virtue of their breadth of vision and the aesthetic of their designs — into the field of future projection: so we have the architectural fancies of Giambattista Piranesi, and in particular the famous *Prisons* which he engraved in 1745; the grandiose projects of Etienne-Louis Boullée in the 1780s (Cénotaphe à Newton); the charcoal drawings of Hugh Ferriss, giving the outlines of a hypothetical Future Metropolis projected forward to the year 1975 (1929); and Frank Lloyd Wright's Mile High Skyscraper, designed in 1956. When one enters the field of visionary architecture, be it that of Boullée, of his contemporary Claude-Nicolas Ledoux, of Tony Garnier (Industrial City, 1917), or of futurist architects such as Antonio Sant'Elia (Futurist City, 1914) and Mario Chiattone, one enters upon a terrain which is Utopian. Their architectural designs — with their tendency to create an overstated and disturbing imaginary world, or one that is totally divorced from the social milieu within which they are supposed to be realised — are conceived within a futurist perspective, ahead

22. *Above: A Soviet engineer imagines the life of the Atlantes who have taken refuge on Mars. 1924*

23. *Right: Le Corbusier's Plan Voisin for the redevelopment of Paris offered a radical vision of the city. 1925*

24. *Facing page, top: Man and machine as seen through the lens of Cartier-Bresson, 1967*

25. *Facing page, bottom: Helix City, Tokyo in the future: a planning scheme by the architect Kurokawa. 1961*

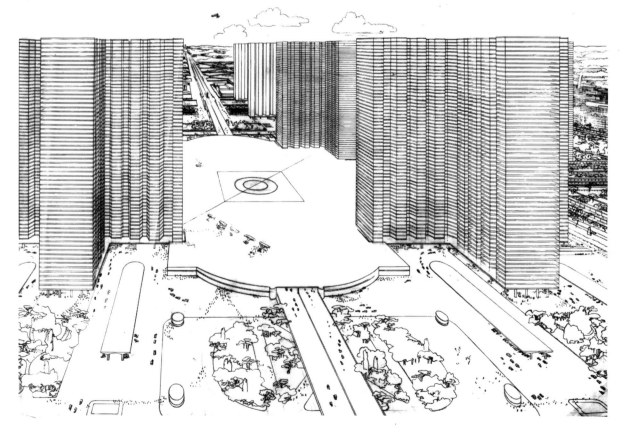

of their time. For Boullée, 'the architect's mission is to orchestrate nature'; in his work, the particular combination of masses, the use of smooth surfaces, the concern with functionality, are summed up in the perfect forms of the sphere and the pyramid, and combine to create an architecture that is made all the more dramatic by the use of light and shade. Ledoux, however, infuses his plans with a spirit of moral and social Utopianism. As for the work of the futurists, 'since there was no notion of their ever being realised, these projects act as simple imaginary evocations destined to stand in their own time as ideological documents of contestation and as statements of a break-away.'[15]

On the other hand, the rationalist architectures of the major twentieth-century theoreticians are only projections of future cities because, in their eyes, the real city is historically backward in relation to the century's advances. The extreme solutions advanced by urbanists are explained by the need to create a modern city commensurate with the development of industry, literature, art and other spheres of civilisation.[16]

Le Corbusier, the high priest of the principle of *tabula rasa* and of Modulor man, argued for drastic modifications in the fabric of the city. Unfortunately, on occasion these were realised, in a bastardised form, and become a future horror being lived in the present, a Utopia gone wrong. 'From his bad seed, badly sown, has sprouted the poisonous fruit of gigantism.'[17] We also note the visual and plastic impact of space-age cities such as the vertical, floating cities of Paul Maymont (1959), the bridge-city of J. Fitzgibbon, K. Kikutake's Marina City, and Kisho Kurokawa's Helix City (1961), which is a plan for a future layout of Tokyo in the form of gigantic spiral towers. All these projects are beautiful objects, extremes of technolatry, but remain unrealised in their radical form.[18]

Evening Comes. The historical futures featured here are, in a sense, the playthings of a lost childhood of Western civilisation. The authors were learning to walk where now we run. These marvellous forgers of reality, as they contrive to transmit images of the future as they hoped it would be, offer us a time voyage in which one climbs aboard the spiral of progress in the same way that one might board the ghost train at a funfair — to play at being tomorrow, to put on a spacesuit, to manipulate directional jet nozzles, to enter houses via the balcony, to warm oneself with radium. Before we finally 'cross the line', we

should go back to yesterday's authors and take a look at their imaginary visions of tomorrow, fed by the knowledge available to them, by their fears and their passions.

In the last decade of the twentieth century, the year 2000 is already being lived as a reality. Around 1850, however, and for a good hundred years afterwards, this date served to crystallise an idealised vision of humanity's mastery of its destiny. The taste for the year 2000, can perhaps be related to the declining force of the myth of America. Obviously, it is easy for these projections into the future to be subjected to *a posteriori* validity checks by experts, and comparisons are inevitable. From the most domestic descriptions of technological perfection to the most far-reaching reshapings of the world and the most radical transformations of modern society and the very essence of humanity, the year 2000 represents a 'vanishing point'. From the most down-to-earth ideal, from the least ambitious of premonitions, to the most adventurous dreams, it is a delayed-action message which cannot permit itself to report that the human species has foundered, that the race has been lost, or that ultimate victory has slipped away.

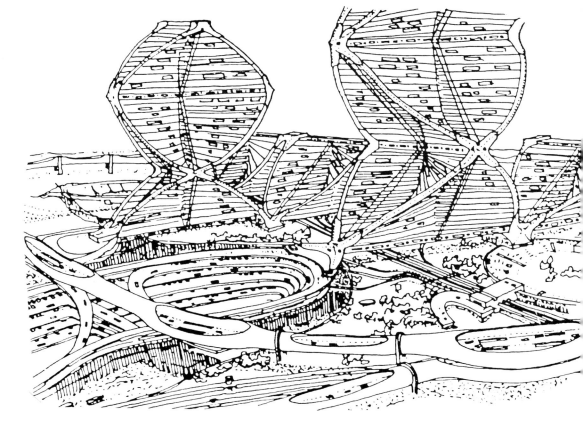

In the rear-vi

Among the authors who offer us prefigurations of the future, not all have chosen to describe the coming millennium. At the end of the nineteenth century, writers were also portraying the likely developments of the twentieth century, and the view was not entirely optimistic. Whatever was going to happen, it promised to be turbulent, although there was also space for visionaries to construct conjectures, extraordinary enough without being far-fetched, and to slip into them the first elements of an improved society. Writers were dazzled by the possibilities of technological progress, and as we trace the threads of what would have happened if history had finally proved them right, we find ourselves dealing with a history which never happened, a history of a totally different century.

ew mirror

It is as if the twentieth century as we have known it never existed. Albert Robida filled its skies with fish-shaped air buses and its streets with well-proportioned feminists, but we know that it has turned out otherwise. Reality has confounded predictions. The present state of the world, in the run-up to the year 2000, contains some traces of what people thought that it was going to be. Reality, events as they have actually happened, are as much the realisation as the negation of the dreams of the previous century. If we go back to the start of the film that presents the prototype of the twentieth century, the images file past like apocryphal memories of hope and of latent anxiety.

Some did not aim as far ahead as the year 2000, but decided that a shorter term would suffice for their prophesies to become reality. Today, the two flows of time — historical and fictional — run alongside each other and mingle, conflict and sometimes repel each other. On the one hand the univocal mass of events that have actually taken place, and on the other the multiform shadows of imagination. An ideal world, or the shipwreck of civilisation — these are the two opposing poles of this one hundred year

perspective. Within this pseudo-history, the twentieth century is constantly portrayed as an era that will be fashioned, for good or ill, by scientific and technological progress.

The Diorama of War. War poisoned the end of the nineteenth century, and people saw it as a cyclical threat which they believed would recur every thirty years. Portrayals of battles in Dorking, Boulogne, Dover, London and Berlin offer a foretaste of real wars to come. Invasions, conquests and wars were envisaged along all the lines that imagination, the actual situation, analysis, anxiety and fear could suggest. The approach of the First World War in 1914 was accompanied by a psychosis about secret invasions from underground, or from the bottom of the sea. Racism appeared in all its hideous guises. The root of evil is within humanity; one has to remember 'what ruthless and utter destruction our own species has wrought, not only upon animals, such as the bison and the dodo, but upon its own inferior races. The Tasmanians, in spite of their human likeness, were entirely swept out of existence in a war of extermination waged by European immigrants, in the space of fifty years.'[1]

Conceived at first as basically involving aircraft, submarines and motor vehicles, the depiction of conflict was to undergo further developments. Reds and anarchists become objects of fear — as, for example, the anarchist miscreant Hartmann. This is the age of the new bandits, the outlaws of the air. The cataclysm of 9 August 1920, unleashed by a series of terrible explosions set off by an organisation of Russian nihilists, provokes an enormous tidal wave which submerges the ancient empire of the Tsars and wipes it off the face of the earth. Other disasters are predicted: a rebellion of the Irish, an invasion by the Blacks, and the ever-present Yellow Peril. But there is also the threat of the Selenians arriving, or the Martians. New York and London are invaded, Paris is blown off the map by an atomic bomb, and the redrawn map of the world has large areas of black on it. In 1874, the British have to fight off a second Armada. England is conquered in May 1852, but also in 1888. We learn that it becomes a republic, and that in the twentieth century it is known as 'the Island of Anarchy'. It was to be the theatre of a civil war in 1915. At a certain point it becomes an underdeveloped country, and Great Britain is

1. Preceding double page: A beautiful evening one weekend in 1980. 1958

2. Left: The war machine of Hartmann the anarchist: the battles of the 20th century will be above all aerial. 1896

3. Top right: The advance guard of the black invasion from Africa. 1919

4. Bottom right: Lethal armoured vehicles in action. 1906

protected by the Blacks of the Sahara in the course of an air battle. In 1940, London burns. In France, people make preparations to repel the imminent invasion of Europe by the Muslim masses of Africa, as plotted by Abdul-M'hamed, a sultan who has been deposed by the English in Constantinople, and who preaches jihad against a Europe that is 'as rotten as those old sycamores that the wind of the South blows over with one gust — rotten in its morals and rotten in its religion'.[2] In 1895 Europe has an emperor named Marmaduke. Newspapers also report a Napoleon IV at the head of the Empire. India is the target of a major Russian invasion in 1879.

To the Slaughterhouse. It goes without saying that war is now world war, total and hellish. Armoured vehicles, tanks, aircraft, submarines and big drilling machines vie with each other in their labours of murderous mining and aggression. Gigantic vacuum cleaners capable of swallowing up entire armies sweep the battlefield. The sky may suddenly be invaded by a squadron of balloons. From their gondolas they release winged troops who begin shooting at a multi-tiered fortress which fires explosive shells back. We gather that it is not uncommon for explosive charges of plutonite to be used. There is also a widespread development of chemical and miasmatic warfare. Lethal gases dropped from special dirigibles, or an air squadron sprays a poison gas which has previously been tested on pigeons. One author reports: 'Within a space of two hours, the Eighth Battalion of Chemists assembles, and lines up with its twenty gleaming batteries, and its troops with their seven days' supply of concentrated meatballs. The medical attack corps arrives in four groups, each with its stock of microbes. At the same time the aerial mobile squadron emerges from its hangar.'[3] The effect of Napus is that anybody it touches is struck by 'anaphasia': there is a sudden flash and the person is dispersed into the ether, leaving nothing behind. New forms of plague also appear, known variously as 'The Scarlet Death', 'The Purple Plague', or simply 'The Plague'. At the time of the Peace Congress in 1909, the engineer Von Satanas was to exhibit his terrifying new weapons. In 1929, fears of gas warfare were such that humanity was forced to live in underground tunnels.

Other military advances derive from electricity, wireless telegraphy and aviation — in particular the prefiguration of so-called 'stealth' aircraft such as the 'invisible warplane' built by the engineers Grahame-White and Harper. Invented in 1915, it was coated with a special paint that made it invisible. It was thought that airships would be extremely useful for night-time navigation, when their task would be to drop 'hundreds of kilos of explosives and incendiary bombs' onto a strategic target, or to fly over enemy armies and

drop 'parachutes carrying powerful lamps' which would expose the enemy to the fire of the opposing army, who would be hidden in darkness.[4] There was also the military use of invisible rays; unlike X-rays, they were transmittable, and would make possible an 'optical telegraphy without any apparent light, which, over short distances, would advantageously replace wireless communications'[5] and would facilitate espionage.

Operation Danger. The size of the stakes and the potential scale of human losses did not escape any of the historians of the century of fire, in which, as they say, 'the god of war went on the march again'. There is a four-day war in 1938. In 1946, in order for peace to be maintained, people have to live in underground cities. In 1954, an Asian invasion overruns Australia. The Japanese attempt to reach New York, but are only able to take the island of Hawaii. Their programme of colonial expansion in Europe dates from as early as 1904. We also have satirical accounts of the future progress of the science of war. 'The first real battle only took place two centuries later, when the Whites used pure persuasion in order to convince the

Yellows to commit mass suicide. Four hundred million Chinese died in the space of an hour, and their government was only able to buy its citizens' right to live at the sixty-second minute, by means of a total surrender.'[6] In 1940, England's Christians are persecuted by the Chinese. The latter, for their part, endure the horrors of civil war in 1951, the crowning moment of which is the sacking of Peking. In Paris, the public is able to watch direct film transmissions of these events on a giant screen, thanks to telephonoscopic communications.

There is also war in the Pacific. The Australo-Mozambican war of 1975 is sparked by a skilful Stock Exchange operation. The course of the war is covered with remarkable accuracy by a French special correspondent, Albert Robida, whose reportage brings him a certain public acclaim. The tactics in the land war involves the use of railways and armoured rolling stock; the air front sees the use of balloons with prototype machine guns, torpedo-grapnels and electric helicopters. Beneath the sea, submarines plumb the ocean depths and launch surprise attacks; and beneath the earth there are battles between electric drilling machines, giant

7. *Taking off from the terrace in a gala aeroplane. 1912*

excavators and borer-torpedoes. But the decisive operations are carried out by means of chemical weapons: the outcome is settled in one day after asphyxiating rockets and shells are fired at the city of Melbourne.

Military conflicts have marked the real twentieth century too deeply for us not to find a muffled trace of them in the fictional histories projecting towards the year 2000 and the eras beyond. According to Maurois, there is a world war in 1947. And the 'Third War' which takes place in 1972 leaves painful memories in people's minds: 'Some men came in a ship many years ago and told us of the terrible events. EMSIAC, hydrogen bombs, radiological dust, supersonic planes. I remember many things. They say Johannesburg was nothing more than a heap of ashes.'[7] Much later, human beings living beneath the earth and on other planets belong to the Intergalactic Organisation of the Great Ring; this troubled period comes to be referred to as the ADN (the Age of Disunited Nations): this characterisation is particularly true of the century which closed the millennium, the century of the Scission, which saw 'the division of the world into two camps. The discovery of the first forms of nuclear energy and obduracy on the part of the supporters of the old regime came close to sparking a terrible catastrophe.'[9]

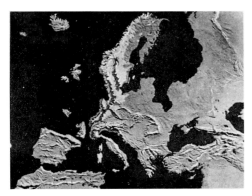 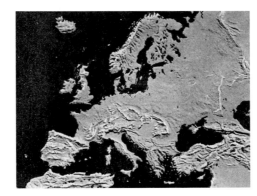

6. *The greenhouse effect and renewed tectonic activity. 1909*

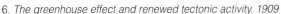

Everything was overwhelmed; when, after several days of storm, calm returned, Russia no longer existed; in its place was a newly-formed ocean. Europe was now an island separated from the Asia of old by a sea that was three hundred leagues wide.

Albert Robida, 1884[8]

8. *Paris and its historic monuments invaded by balloons. 1883*

A historian of the year 3750 notes that one of the salient events dividing the two eras was the discovery of nuclear energy and the dropping of the first atomic bomb. The absolute weapon, the unnamable weapon, the supreme explosive is now in humanity's hands. An unknown aggressor drops nuclear bombs which exterminate seventy million Americans; the survivors, hidden in underground tunnels, set out to find the aggressor and destroy him. In other stories we learn that nuclear war did not actually take place; people woke up believing that they could hear bombs, but the bombs never actually fell. The historian adds: 'What we had here was a necessary stage: it was necessary for humanity to go to the limits of its perversity so that it could end by loathing it, and instead embark on the search for wisdom.'[10]

Universal Energy. Another recurrent and dominant image of the twentieth century is that of total personal and social fulfilment. Comfort and a life of idleness. We can sit in our armchairs and watch electricity doing everything for us: 'It will cook our

One day it will be realised that X-rays are a mystification.
Lord Kelvin, 1895[11]

9. *The country house with an ascending pavilion is a bourgeois privilege. 1883*

dinner, sew on our buttons, write our letters, make our clothes, beat our children, black our boots, shave our stubbly chins, and even help us to a pinch of snuff, if we want some. We believe it will eventually reach such perfection as to carry us up to bed, undress us, tuck us up, and blow out the candle, when we are too tired, or weary, to do it ourselves.'[12]

Given that everything runs on steam, or electricity, or nuclear energy, houses don't need servants, factories don't need workers, and the countryside doesn't need animals. The picture is of a life that is greatly simplified, authoritarian and regulated in its smallest details: food, clothing, fertility, culture and transport. All problems, or virtually all, can be resolved by technology; everything provides a pretext for invention. Innovation is the order of the day, be it in the kitchen, or in transportation, as in this description of a vehicle which is a cross between a ship and a balloon: 'The interior of Shell-32 comprises a vast living-room, as well as a library and smoking room, six bedrooms, a dining room, a kitchen, the crew's quarters, a bathroom, and an engine room operating on liquid air, which provides power, heating and lighting. The craft is armed with two machine guns; there are also two dismantled reserve aeroplanes on board, and a powerful automobile.'[13] However, in the depths of the pre-1914-18 slump, mechanisation is no longer extolled so eagerly, and one begins to see it portrayed as a harbinger of apocalyptic times. With a new century beginning to rise up out of the ruins of the old world, Albert Robida denounces the disasters of Electricity, that malevolent goddess.

Leisure a Go-Go. When you go to the theatre, plays are performed simultaneously in three languages. Theatre and music may be relayed to your home, as may parliamentary debates. If you have a telephone subscription to theatrical reviews, you're likely to find a succession of night-time despatches disturbing your sleep unless you've remembered to press the 'stop' button. Advertising is turned into literature and sent down the telephonograph. People use aerial bungalows made out of cardboard and chipboard for their holidays by the sea and elsewhere. There are occasional unfortunate accidents due to forgotten torpedoes, the dangerous relics of the Great Universal War of 1910; however, the shipwrecked can always swim to safety on the man-made islands which serve as refuges out at sea. The Louvre museum in Paris is visited by means of an internal tram system.

10. *A suspended aerial train leaving Strasbourg station. 1905*

11. *Enjoying the cancan in your own home by telephonoscope. 1883*

Death to Books. Literature gets a very bad press. The classics are subjected to a process of radical concentration: 'Each author is summed up in a mnemonic doggerel, which can be swallowed painlessly and remembered with no effort.'[14] The passing of the law of 22 September 1943 by the World Parliament, ordering the destruction of all written matter, creates a situation where 'nobody in the world reads anything any more, except brief, hasty and ephemeral shorthand notes relating to the material details of existence, but which an honest man would have blushed to use for more noble purposes. And, to tell the truth, nobody thought any longer that such a thing was possible.'[15] At the same time, sadly, every sphere of cultural life on earth is invaded by a universal mishmash of language, and an audio-visual dictatorship destroys privacy and splatters its inhuman images across a giant screen. On rainy days, pedestrians are invited to hire preprinted pictures to carry on the sides of their walking shelters.

'The twentieth century will be happy. Nothing of the old history will remain: people will no longer need to fear conquest, invasion, usurpation, armed conflict, an interruption of civilisation occasioned by marriages between royal families, a division of nations by congress, a dismemberment occasioned by the passing of dynasties . . .' Victor Hugo had invested the twentieth century with a Utopian hope, and this section from *Les Misérables* ends on a note which is indirectly prophetic: 'One might almost be in a position to say: there will be no history — people will be happy.' When, under Stalin, historical figures of communism suddenly began to be erased from photographs, when attempts were made to make them disappear from history, and when George Orwell demonstrated in *1984* the pernicious efficacy of large-scale disinformation, everything seemed to be heading broadly in the same direction, except that there was a lack of agreement on what exactly was going to comprise happiness in the twentieth century. In order to remake history, all that was needed was to erase the event in question.

Public opinion is manipulated by the big newspaper owners, the five Dictators of Opinion, who come to an agreement among themselves to avoid new carnage. They are a Frenchman, an Englishman, a German, an American and a Japanese.[16] Their mendacious press campaign was to end in the unleashing of an interplanetary war. On 17 April 1975 a Stock Exchange crash was triggered by the arrival of a time traveller.

12. *Notre-Dame cathedral in Paris converted into a metropolitan balloon station. 1905*

An Ideal Society. Paris, in 1952, comprises 64 arrondissements and extends all along the Seine as far as Rouen. Changes in government are strictly organised by means of regular revolutions or by ten-year periods of enforced absence of one of the parties. We see the Bastille being taken for a second time, having been rebuilt in bricks, plaster and canvas, and we are introduced to a World Exposition of barricades in 1953. There are courses in political parliamentary technique, which teach the art of attacking or praising your opponents. Everything is available, at a price, from parliamentary legislation to pornography. Aerial robbers are caught and searched by the atmosphere police, and criminals are lodged in a penitentiary out in the countryside, where they are rehabilitated by means of kindness. A food factory supplies meals directly to your home. An automatic bill-poster pastes up proclamations, concert programmes and advertisements. Immortality has now been achieved, so that people no longer look their age, and a sensible man, thinking that a way is needed to distinguish the young from the old, suggests that people should be given registration numbers. As and when people do die, express trains take their bodies to incinerator factories located on the edge of the North Sea.

However H. G. Wells had warned the dreamers: 'A World State, therefore, it must be. That leaves no room for a modern Utopia in Central Africa, or in South America, or round about the pole, those last refuges of idealism. The floating island of La Cité Morellyste no longer avails. We need a planet.'[17] We find that Boston is the home of organised socialist society. A socialist revolution takes place in London in 1888, and after a period of socialist government the monarchy is restored in 2000. A sixth continent is officially inaugurated on 1 January 1960; it is created by putting together the archipelagos, islands and atolls of Polynesia into a huge landmass which is known as Helenia.

The March of the Suffragettes. Some pioneering women had drawn attention to themselves early on through their writings and their outrageously liberated lifestyles. Discarding their long dresses, women began by shortening their skirts, then wore gaiters, and ended up wearing trousers and a masculine style of

13. *Above: Big Brother is Watching You. 1955*

14. *Below: Liberated from work, man is replaced by agricultural robots. 1896*

In 1960, work will be limited to three hours per day.

John Langdon-Davies, 1936[19]

It is generally accepted that by 1980, ships, aeroplanes, locomotives and even cars will be fuelled by atomic energy.

General David Sarnoff, 1955[18]

dress: 'Women's skirts were extremely short, worn over culottes of silk velvet and leggings made of Russian leather embroidered with arabesques.'[20] During the reign of Karyl the Great, the revolt of 1920-22 ends with the passing of a law of equality between the sexes. From now on, emancipation meant that women could both vote and be elected, and the honour of being the first female Member of Parliament fell to Martha Brown. Whether they were lawyers or bankers, women had serious-sounding first names. Needlework was banned, and consequently had to be done in secret.

Needless to say, after the no-birth strike, women no longer raise their own children, this work being taken in hand by the State. Babies are fed collectively by steam-powered feeding. Sometimes, as in 1948, as a result of the overenthusiastic application of Malthusian principles, we find a shortage of children, so national maternity hospitals have to be set up. These are full-time baby factories. There are plans to ban celibacy, and to tax it at a rate proportional to the age of the person concerned. In London a kind of obligatory Mormonism is in force, which involves, among other things, marriage warehouses

15. *A trip in the night skies above Paris. 1883*

From now on, man can do whatever he wants, technologically. Frank Borman, 1962[21]

16. *Mid-season women's fashion in 1952. 1883*

and prison for bachelors. We learn that each town has its Marriage Avenue and that marriage adverts hang from the stage curtains of theatres. A law of 1932 lays down the number of children that couples are expected to provide to the State, as from the first year of marriage, and in the years thereafter.

Rule by women is predicted by more than one author. It is political, tyrannical and unlivable, and appears in 1930, 1940 and 2002 — but may be projected as far forward as 2174 or 2525. Here we have an updated version of the ancient theme of the world turned upside down. Fortunately, the writer's pen is often guided by humour, as, in 1953, when the warriors of the 'Battalion of Female Supremacy Arriving at the Barricades' appear. Couples whose marriage is on the rocks are advised to use domestic telegraphy, while young girls are courted via telephonoscopes. The basic structure of the family remains unchanged, and does not develop down the path of single-parent families and broken homes.

17. *Right: Aero-taxis require skilful handling in the confused skies of the capital. 1890*

18. *On paper, everyone has been to the moon long before 1969. 1883*

Some proclaim that marriage will disappear, and that love will come to be seen as a sickness. They predict that a revolt of women will bring about a reduction in, and then an abolition of, the male gender. Utopian matriarchy is almost always a synonym for oppression, and can develop as far as rule solely by the female sex, made possible by means of parthenogenesis. Jean Rostand evoked this possibility: 'Are we perhaps not far from the day when human beings will be born without fathers? What will they look like? Everything suggests that they will belong to the female sex, and that they will be identical with their mothers: rather like younger twin sisters.'[22]

No Pedestrian Right of Way. James Gillray and other English caricaturists suggested, in around 1825, that the march of progress (*The March of Intellect*) would take place under the sign of the air balloon, and when aircraft come to replace balloons in about 1910, the most common vision of the twentieth century is of a society dynamised by air transport. Soldiers, postmen, strollers, housewives and courting couples are variously decked out with wings, parachutes and propellors; they ride on bicycles with inflated elytrons, in balloons with anchors, in small aircraft and dirigibles. Given the spread of air travel, domestic architecture is necessarily transformed. Concierges have their cubbyholes next to the arrival hall on the roof. The important thing that a visitor needs to know is how to step over the balcony with a decisive, confident air.

People rarely travel at ground level, but if they do, then they go very fast, on moving pavements, and never like ex-pedestrians. High-speed pneumatic tubes provide an ideal means of travelling from Madrid to Tangiers, or from one end of town to the other. The same system is also used in big department stores for transporting parcels and customers. Like many other international spectacles, we find the aerial balloon race between Oxford and Tokyo being broadcast in Moscow in 1962. Rail transport is transformed: trains run on monorails, or are suspended in mid-air, or mounted on runners. They also travel at high speed down flat rails from which they are separated by a jet of water.[23] Paris to Bordeaux in 45 minutes! Cities are criss-crossed with commuter railways, and trains buzz round famous monuments like flies round a jam pot. In 1947 we find a submarine expedition being organised to the North Pole. Some submarines are equipped for flight, and for travelling on land. In 1927, Lt. Anthony 'Buck' Rogers is trapped in a rock-slide, and falls asleep for 500 years.

Shivers. As in all epochs, there is something of a sense of the end of the world. In 1992, a new planet comes dangerously close to earth. In 1950, Mars is cut in two, leading to the creation of a triple universe. In 1985, the inhabited countries of the earth are submerged by a terrible Ice Age.

And the moon! The moon is truly the symbol of our twentieth century. So close, so familiar, it has long held an attraction for the bold and the brave. The view from the sphere carrying Cavor and Bedford causes the narrator to cry out: 'We couldn't see anything but the moon, a stupendous scimitar of white dawn with its edge hacked out by notches of darkness, the crescent shore of an ebbing tide of darkness, out of which peaks and pinnacles rose up in the brilliant light of the sun.'[24] Other travellers followed them.

The Count of Mars reached Mars in 1916, and as a result the planet was added to the colonies of the British monarchic republic. A famous expert pronounces that 'trips to the moon, Mars and Venus will be commonplace by 1977'.[25]

19. *Departure from Paris in a European express pneumatic tube. 1883*

It was in the year 1950 that a new Christopher Columbus, already long announced by the story-tellers, boarded our satellite. Only a Frenchman could have had the boldness. Octave Béliard, 1910 [26]

An ordi day in

nary the year 2000

In its futuristic versions, everyday life is not so very different from life as we know it. It is portrayed in simple, human terms, expressing people's desire to enjoy a life of comfort and the pleasures of a small, clean and modern home of their own. Engineers will have applied their energies to satisfying our needs and filling our lives with gadgets.

They will have fashioned a positive technology for the use of everyone, although nowadays it seems that it was less important to explain its functioning principles than to proclaim the state of well-being that could be attained from its services. The year 2000 provided an ideal reassurance for the aspirations of the new middle class; they would have appreciated having somebody else to take care of the important things in life, orchestrating their fate and leaving them to worry only about the incidentals.

The future worlds imagined are numerous and come in all shapes and sizes. They range from the optimistic, through the dynamic, the wait-and-see and the sceptical, to the pessimistic. These tomorrows are closed and independent worlds; they are also unalterable, because they will never actually be realised. However, at the moment of their creation they are true; the day which will render them obsolete is still in the distance. Furthermore, they share one characteristic: their concern to describe and to evoke in its smallest details the realities — the supposed realities — of life in the future.

It is at the level of the everyday that one best perceives the temporal changes: the lines of a motor car, the cut of an item of clothing, the shapes of the objects people use. These details provide a yardstick demarcating the *passé* from the futurist. This is why Robida gives his women short skirts, and sheaths the legs of his beautiful heroines in striped or chequered stockings; elsewhere chairs may have top-shaped or slender, tapering legs; cars and spacecraft tend to be egg-shaped or pointed. But all these forays into the future are fairly sober, and content themselves with giving an image of a future which is in fact a

today in disguise: the technique is to take things that exist in embryo in a given epoch, magnify them by the use of humour, fantasy and imagination, and transpose them ten, twenty or a hundred years into the future. And there we find that nothing has changed. Apart from minor details, everything about everyday life is basically the same; children still go to school, servants and delivery boys still go about their business, and there are burglars and courting couples. However the children have their own personal teachers, are taught at home, and may use listening devices and records instead of books; servants may be replaced by machines; delivery boys do their rounds in dirigibles; and courting couples are the same as they have always been, except that one is as likely to find them in the air as on *terra firma*.

When authors at the start of the twentieth century sought to foresee the realities of the year 2000, they took the most recent inventions, the most amazing discoveries of the era, and transposed them into the future. These inventions, having only just been made, were the privilege of a handful of pioneers or specialists, but in the hands of our authors they suddenly become familiar, everyday objects.

1. *Preceding double page: Seduction amid the skyscrapers, or 'aeromance'. 1930*

2. *Left: The automatic barber of the future. 1890*

3. *Right: Taking things easy in the butler's pantry. 1906*

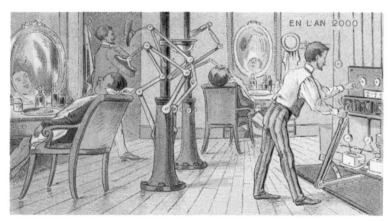

4. *Variations on daily life in the comfort of a carefree year 2000. 1910*

5. *Elegant aerial women after a night at the opera. 1902*

A Life of Ease. Food, clothing, travel, communications and living space — these are the prime terrain onto which Mr Everyman's future is extrapolated, along lines that are reassuring, efficient and precise. Life in the future is portrayed as *a priori* easier, more interesting and in every way better than present-day life, with which it is sometimes directly compared. Thus, in 1905, an idyllic vision inspired by the English garden cities is counterposed 'to the stone hives into which the masses are crammed nowadays'. In this vision, 'the entire country will become one enormous city, or rather an immense park, scattered with delightful villas, which will be surrounded by trees and flowers, and, here and there, "ganglionic" focal points where public services will be concentrated.'[1] At a later date, one's food requirements may be provided as follows: 'In boarding a jet aircraft for a journey to the antipodes, one will only need to take a tiny case packed with pills which will represent three months-worth of rations.'[2] Some people prefer not to indulge, since they fear that their digestive apparatuses might atrophy; however, one can always hold one's nose and down some 'soyaburger and

In the cluttered skies of modern cities, dirigibles with propellors and similar fantasies emerge from the worlds of Santos-Dumont and Count Zeppelin. The 'Voisin' aeroplane, piloted by Henri Farman, as well as Santos-Dumont's 'Demoiselle' and the Wright Brothers' aircraft, features in air races alongside implausible aircraft with bats' wings, inspired by Ader's 'Aeolus'. If it's not an aerocab that one takes to travel the skies, then it's an omnibus-balloon, or a winged hackney carriage, or a specially designed cannonball. But this near and almost tangible future is not at all disturbing; science fiction invades everyday life to the point of becoming completely normal and unsurprising.

Think of the inefficiency of a hundred thousand houses for a hundred thousand families as compared with a hundred-thousand-unit Section; a book-film collection in each house as compared with a Section film concentrate; independent video for each family as compared with video-piping systems. For that matter, take the simple folly of endless duplication of kitchens and bathrooms as compared with the thoroughly efficient diners and shower rooms made possible by city culture. Isaac Asimov, 1953 [3]

6. *Standardised food and assembly line meals. 1947*

7. The arrival of an aerial transatlantic liner on the roof of a New York skyscraper. 1910

regenerated steak'.[4] Filmed books, 'sensi-cinema', 3-D, hypervideo and hypnotic films will fill people's leisure time and satisfy their desire to escape from reality. Biblio-technicians will, on demand, supply every conceivable kind of information, with the aid of electronic memory-machines. There will be an extraordinary variety of means of transport, including the Ara-chnians, high-speed vehicles capable of reaching speeds of between 25 and 35 kilometres per hour. Amazing!

Extrapolators into the future may limit themselves to a leap of only fifteen or twenty years in order to describe the everyday life of the future. Beyond that limit, the adventurers of the future scorn verisimilitude and probability; they prefer to play on fantasy and humour within a framework of the dis-coveries of their time. Out in the streets one finds robot-vendors, a highly developed kind of walking automatic distributor: 'The lower part of Robie's body consisted of a metal hemisphere, edged with foam rubber, which reached down almost to the pavement. The upper part was a metal box containing dark holes. The box was able to pivot and lean. It looked like a crinoline dress with a little turret

Before each diner was a complex apparatus of porcelain and metal. There was one plate of white porcelain, and by means of taps for hot and cold volatile fluids the diner washed this himself between the courses; he also washed his elegant white metal knife and fork and spoon as occasion required. Soup and the chemical wine that was the common drink were delivered by similar taps, and the remaining covers travelled in tastefully arranged dishes down the table along silver rails. H. G. Wells, 1899[5]

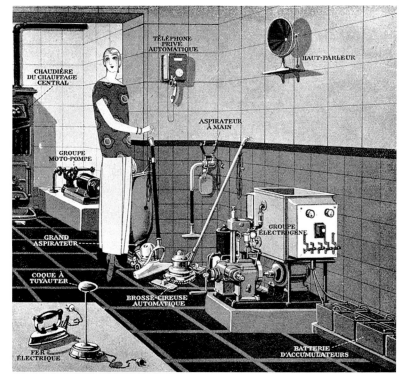

8. Domestic appliances will liberate the modern woman. 1924

on top.'[6] Even more sophisticated are the telepathic personal assistants who see to your comfort and save you time and effort. These are the 'peepers' — experts in extra-sensory perception. 'His peeper secretary knew where he was going. His peeper chauffeur knew where he wanted to go. Reich arrived in his apartment and was met by his peeper butler who at once announced early luncheon and dialled the meal to Reich's unspoken demands.'[7]

Extrapolation: Bold Deductions.

Technological invention and scientific discovery are the bedrock of run-of-the-mill extrapolations. At this level, there is no need for a censorship imposed by the demands of realism. If electricity is universal, then it is obvious that everything will run on electricity: trains, brains and cannons included. If men have succeeded in piloting flying machines, then the imaginations of their contemporaries are to be conquered by predictions of a future world where the most mundane of everyday activities will take place in flight. The appearance of isotopes, X-rays and transistors will exercise a similar seduction on later generations of artists.

The wealth of descriptive, anecdotal and often over-precise detail tends to be matched by a poverty of intuition, or a calculated lack of interest in the details of the hardware of the future, which is anyway irrevocably destined for early obsolescence. The time machine of Wells's time traveller is an extremely simple device. Moreover, the claim to have achieved a degree of progress becomes facile when the intermediary stages between the state of knowledge of one's own epoch and that required to accomplish the various technological wonders described in futuristic novels are either not described, left vague, or brushed aside with a pseudo-scientific jargon. Thus we have astronauts landing on the moon with equipment which is patently laughable: 'They were able to communicate with each other electrically by means of thin wires and plugs, which were connected to sockets mounted on the sides of their helmets. This enabled them to talk to each other; in addition they had a dry-cell telephone operating in their craft. They also had electric lamps suspended from their belts, protected by a metal tube and a wire grille, and attached to a flexible wire.'[8]

All these futurist elements relate to a grammar of forms which is declined and articulated by means of images; forms which, moreover, are subject to a variable coefficient of uselessness, of inappropriateness, which is easy for us to identify today. When these forms were created by their illustrators, in 1883, 1910, 1928, 1954 or 1961, they were charged with evoking and symbolising for their contemporaries an image of the year 2000, or some other period of the future. They have produced archetypes which are subject to three main constants: an amplification of function, movement-as-king, and an enormity of scale — constants which underlie the principal headings of the catalogue of the future.

But these images and texts almost never deceive their reader, whether contemporary or not. The discrepancy with reality is perceived, mainly by virtue of 'displaced' details — in other words, details located outside the frame of reference, which is the here and now of the anticipator. These details speak of a 'here, but in a future time', or of an 'elsewhere and in another time'. As a result, the descriptions and the illustrations end up in a state of more or less apparent hybridisation: women walk on Venus in lace-up ankle boots and long skirts, kitted out with rubbery masks; storms blow up over the sea which has submerged what was once the Sahara desert; Romeo and Juliet sing on the stage of a classical Italian-style theatre, but they are accompanied by a pneumatico-mechanico-electrico-symphonic orchestra. Lifts move by means of anti-gravity, and if you happen to forget to lock your toes under the specially provided bars, people will take you for a provincial as you float around in the cabin.[9] Elsewhere, well-behaved children play croquet at the bottom of the sea; Notre-Dame in Paris has big banners hung between its two towers advertising the sales; and an entire room — people, cat, dog, furniture and flowers — floats in a state of weightlessness between ceiling and floor. Authors vie with each other in the description of styles, ranging from formalism to exuberance, but the more fantastical styles are the most enchanting: 'What wonderful long trains, mounted on little metal rollers which hummed deliciously on the sand! What hats, with their tangled vines, tree-like plants, tropical birds, snakes and miniature jaguars, of which a Brazilian forest would have given but an imperfect idea! What chignons, of such a weight and volume that these elegant women were obliged to carry them in little wicker baskets.'[10]

9. Long-distance cannonballs for airborne passengers in the world as it will be. 1845

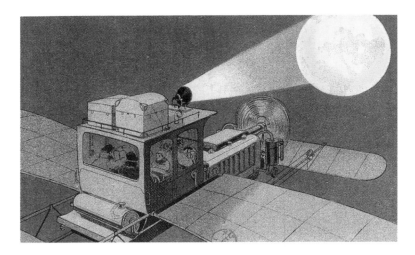

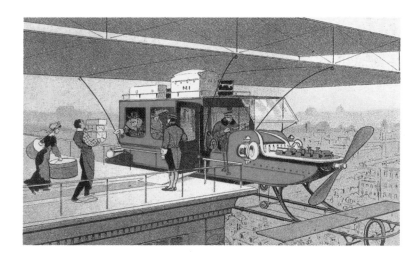

10. *Scenes from life in the year 2012, to be tasted with a bar of chocolate. 1912*

11. *Paris-Nord: intersection for car, air and rail traffic. 1935*

Catalogue of the Future. Life in the future is so colourful, so exuberant, so various as it is portrayed by successive writers that it is hard to grasp in its entirety. The images are invasive, swarming and busy. In the midst of this variety, one element stands out: an irrepressible optimism. Writers were confident that the future was going to be radiant, marvellous, amazing, technological and, above all, infallible. It's a smiling world where even the convicts are happy. 'Me, my jet-car, my robot and my wife.' Physical needs are foreseen and satisfied: 'Decent furniture, guaranteed to give perfect comfort, a drinks cabinet, and screens connected to a huge audio-visual library.'[11] Whether it's a question of polishing the parquet, dressing madame, bathing the baby, measuring sir when he wants a new suit, or even building a house, machines are there, efficient, attentive, and perfectly regulated. In 2889, an American journalist abandons himself to the mercies of his mechanical dresser, and 'two minutes later, without him needing to call on the services of the valet, the machine had washed him, combed his hair, put on his shoes, dressed him, buttoned him from head to toe and deposited him at the door to his office' — at the *Earth Herald* located on 16823 Avenue.[12] Machines can be relied upon to prepare a meal — either chemical or ordinary — to perform a concert, to oversee the intensive and accelerated breeding of

Inside the house was an automatic scrub bath. The dining room produced dishes of warm food from its interior in response to commands, which it acknowledged. All communications were televised. Each room was telepathic, catching emanations and creating whatever was desired. There were no stairs. People walked into an air closet and a draught sucked them up to the next floor. Shoe-tier, toothcleaner, hair-brusher, picture-painter, suction-mail tube were limbs of this extraordinary creature. The house itself became wife, mother and nursemaid to everyone inside it.
John Atkins, 1958 [13]

selected poultry, to guarantee a flawless education of docile young minds, or to tailor a made-to-measure suit. Needless to say, electricity rules, and there's hardly an inch of wall which isn't blinking with luminous buttons, indicators of a ceaseless activity. Machines are capable of carrying out the work of a hundred workers; the illumination of an entire city; communication with the Antipodes, or Mars, or the National Assembly; or recording a disc-cheque at the bank.

The bibliophone, 'a sort of phonograph which reads out loud pre-recorded texts', is a handy tool for the Kentropolitans, because they are all short-sighted by virtue of their avidity for study.[14] Mechanical writing devices and thought helmets will become more widespread; people will learn to read by means of a brain operation carried out on their 'Reading Day'; and the discovery of the brain's mechanisms for storing knowledge will mean that each individual will be provided with the education that best suits him.[15]

Elsewhere, people will spend their lives with miniature radios inserted in their ears — small sound shells pouring out 'an electronic ocean of sounds, music and words'; in people's houses there may be broadcasts

transmitted through screens on the walls.[16] There will be replaceable platinum brains, and back-up brains will be installed in people's hats. It will be impossible to get lost, even if, for example, you've only just landed in the immense galactic astroport of Trantor for the first time. Holding a slightly phosphorescent ticket, you set off in the direction indicated: 'Follow the light. The ticket will keep glowing as long as you're pointed in the right direction.'[17]

Omnibus cars are properly heated in winter and kept dust-free, and the streets are paved with blocks of porphyry.[18] Statuesque bodies, showing no trace of old age, are kneaded, burnished, plucked, vacuum-massaged and maintained by pneumatic surgery. Fashion has not lost its importance, and despite a tendency towards standardisation of clothing, metallic bras and other body-hugging accessories will eliminate any attempt at uniformisation between the sexes. Some preach nudity, others prefer low necklines and cut-outs.

And what about fuel sources? 'Small atomic generators installed in people's homes will provide sufficient energy for a lifetime, without needing to be recharged.'[19] Elsewhere, people will use means of transport moving at 'between 200 and 250 kilometres per hour; trains will make the journey from Paris to Marseilles in under four hours! This will involve travelling on an overhead cable. The railways of the future will be monorails, suspended in the air and running on electricity.'[20] Someone else predicts railways will be abandoned in favour of air transport. Motor vehicles will be expected to observe minimum speed limits; slow drivers and pedestrians will risk being sent to prison.[21]

12. *Top: A martyr of female emancipation. 1947*

13. *Right: The city of Boston in the 21st century.*

It is not only plausible, but even natural to think that in the relatively near future travellers will prefer to use aerial means of transport, rather than terrestrial. Aerial stations and landing points will give a picturesque and unexpected aspect to our present-day cities. **Alberto Santos-Dumont, 1905**[22]

14. *Above: Hugo Gernsback predicts what daily life will be like in the year 2660. 1929*

15. *Right: Anti-gravitation at home. 1920*

Moving pavements, now ubiquitous, provide the pleasure of speed, running at between eight and twenty-four kilometres per hour. Others go even faster, and travellers step off accelerator belts onto secondary belts, and then onto the express, which travels at more than a hundred kilometres per hour. Adolescents race each other along these conveyors, and regard this dangerous and forbidden game as a form of sport.[23] The use of 'jumpers' or anti-gravity devices will become so commonplace that everybody will have one. 'They were belts, strapped high under the arms, containing an amount of inertron appropriate to the wearer's weight and purposes. In effect they made a man weigh as little as he wished; two pounds if he liked.'[24] Progress may also mean hailing an aero-cab, or driving a personal travel module, or leaving on an aerial holiday, or landing on the roof of your house in an aeroplane, or cultivating gardens suspended below a helicopter, or going to London in a flying car, or taking the legendary Calais-Dover tunnel or the new European tube. One writer imagined 'a rocket-aircraft, suitably fitted out, which could carry passengers with ease out beyond the denser layers of the atmosphere, into the stratosphere where the more rarefied air will require much less power from the craft, making it easier to reach other planets.'[25] Progress also means aerodynamics, moving from hymenopteras and dirigibles with bat-shaped wings to craft as perfectly streamlined as a knife-blade. Bicycles will also be streamlined, and will be pedalled horizontally. Monorail trains will be built according to the laws of ballistics, as will submarines. Thinking of crossing the Atlantic? You need only catch the New York aerosteamer, which will touch down on the terrace of a Parisian hotel. Others prefer alternative means of transport: a particular favourite is the steam-powered submarine, known as the 'dolphin express'. One author observes that the 'submarine tubes by means of which one can travel from Europe in two hundred and ninety-five minutes, are infinitely preferable to the aero-trains, which are limited to a thousand kilometres per hour'.[26]

There is no point in asking questions. At any moment, for any situation in everyday life, solutions exist. Floating islands emerge in the middle of oceans; giant screens magnify the image of a speaker in public squares; press headlines projected onto the terraces of big public buildings are visible from an aerial omnibus; and advertisements extend across the clouds or appear on the sides of balloons. In enormous tower-cities, great tower blocks provide both offices and living space, and you move up the building as you are promoted. At certain levels the stair landings are peopled by nocturnal lodgers who are kept at bay by automatic barriers.[27] A Roman-style aqueduct is built in order to provide home deliveries of cabbage soup to an entire population.

Suspended from overhead rails, passenger trains will race along, unhindered, at incredible speeds.

Je sais tout, 1905[28]

16. *Top: Project for a flying caravan. 1912*

17. *Right: The streets are lit by iridium and pedestrians move around autonomously. 1929*

18. *Facing page: New sports cars will hurtle down streets at unheard of speeds. 1934*

Some people resist change, but change is relentless: 'You push a button, and extraordinary things happen. Electric eye, tone selector, discs that can be played on both sides, accompanied by all kinds of weird noises ... You probably understand these things. I don't. Every time I put a Crosby record in a supermachine like that, poor Bing seems embarrassed.'[29]

Operating Instructions for the Future. The future, which has already been defined as qualitatively superior to the here and now, is depicted through snapshots of life. There is nothing in them which is disturbing, because the imbalances that are present and assumed are not actually described. Life in the future is a succession of practical questions, for which a precise answer is proposed.

There seems to be no place for shade. Whether one is at the top of huge tower blocks or on an aerial footbridge, or at the wheel of a flying car, or inside a train tearing along a submarine tunnel, the environment is always illuminated. Either the sun or powerful luminous panels create an eternal day. In extreme cases, there is no point in having stars: nature has disappeared from the cities, and beneath their sheltering domes it is always daytime.

Life may be less ordered than one might like to think; in these enclosed, protected anthills, there are sometimes shortages of places for people to live, and water is so precious that after five minutes the fresh water in your shower gives way to salt water. When you go out in the street, you have to wear anti-dust masks, and only your standardised leisure timetable gives you a sense of what time of day it is. People no longer pay in local money; everyone pays by 'credits'. What about the unconscious? There is no place for it; dreams have been tamed. At home you will have a computer, and it will have answers for everything, since it is linked to all existing memory banks. 'Anything that you want to know, you key it in, and it comes. That's how you solve your problems — it fulfils the role of chemist, doctor, physicist, astronomer and a teller of good stories.'[30]

In the future world, the present is transposed, dressed up in bizarre forms and novel inventions, so as to provide an illustration of progress in its pure state. Progress? Progress means producing, producing and producing. It will be built on 'the industrialisation of agronomy, which is still so empirical and rudimentary; the limitless improvement of agricultural machinery and processes; a collaboration between chemists

19. *At any time of the day, pressing a button will solve any problem, satisfy any desire. 1930*

and electricians; methodical irrigation; a rational selection of seeds.'[31] Chlorellae — highly nourishing protein-filled seaweed — will be intensively cultivated. There will also be good results from food plants which have been rendered polyploid (i.e., carrying more than two kinds of chromosomes in the nucleus of the cell) by the application of biology or radioactivity: 'A radioactive cobalt-firing device is installed in a field. It is also possible to hang small radioactive cobalt

appliances from the branches of trees, in order to expose the buds of apple trees, for example, or of other fruit trees, to radiation.'[32]

Problems which may arise at an archaeological, demographic or ecological level are rather ignored, since all change is seen as positive. In the field of medicine, it is commonplace to find refrigerated cabinets packed with 'living corpses' ready to supply replacement organs; operations are carried out with ultrasonic scalpels or

20. *Left: One happily removes one's spacesuit to be less formal. 1953*

21. *Right: A beautiful lady being cared for by her hairdresser-beautician-robot in the year 2000. 1955*

electric 'pencils', which are clean, aseptic and anaesthetising.[33] The duration of life has been enormously extended, and people's bodies are regularly cleansed of accumulations of entropy by 'energy-cleaning: a chemical and radioactive washing of the organism, accompanied by wave stimulation'.[34] Sometimes people realise that they have gone too far down the road of perfection, and that life loses its value when machines rule everything; at that point people back off: 'I knew now that anything could happen. The security hatches had been closed. Illnesses had been freed. With hope, luck and love I could live for a thousand years. Or I could die tomorrow. I was free.'[35]

The future comes across as a civilisation of the ersatz: robot salespeople, robot café waiters, hydroponic food, pigmentation pills, clothes made of kerato-fibre, legs sheathed in skylon, drugs that are able to stimulate the emotions and induce happiness. There are two constants in these visions of everyday life in the future: first, these are descriptions of worlds that are finished, completed, and 'perfect', and thus close to Utopias — worlds in which the immobility of individuals — fed, clothed and amused — mirrors the immobility of the societies in question, which are fully formed, productive and happy. Communications and transport are rapid — and so are the extrapolations themselves, which vie with each other to impose what they see as their unique and definitive vision; in so doing, once again they return to a closed world. The dynamic of time has fled in the face of this theatre where authors recite the same piece over and over again, alongside other authors, on narrow, parallel stages.

Futurist Clichés. Predigested culture, balanced meals, rational housing — life is very simple and rather uniform. There is a concern to reduce causes of friction to a minimum. People live a rhythm of arbitrary time-cycles, and they lose the habit of fresh air, sunshine and blue skies. There is no question of breaking out of the routine, and of dreaming of sleeping anywhere other than on a 'wire mattress with pneumatic cushions inflated with temperature-controlled air'.[36] One might also sleep 'in space, or more precisely on a radiation mattress which maintains the sleeper at a height of fifty centimetres above the bed',[37] and the heat of the radiation may be controlled, as desired. If one prefers a change of scenery, some bedrooms have the ability to create an illusion of being in the countryside. The edges of the room may become indistinct, or may even disappear; above the bed a square of blue water spreads over a panel which you have to examine closely, 'to be sure that there really isn't water splashing from one side to the other'.[38] Woken by the glow of his multi-function clock, man gets up from his temperature-controlled 'hydropathic' bed.[39] On the planet Mars, sleep comes once one has stretched out on a 'soft carpeting of mist that poured from the walls when she lay down to rest'.[40]

But the telepathic house, the robot house, comes from further ahead than the year 2000. This house 'spoke, thought, listened, acted, entertained. The walls could dissolve into a three-dimensional scene of jungle or

22. *As buildings get higher and higher, people will get around on multi-level transparent streets. 1932*

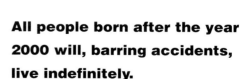

All people born after the year 2000 will, barring accidents, live indefinitely.

Arthur C. Clarke, 1962[41]

veldt, anything you liked, a scene from a fairy tale or from a romance, with animals and vegetation to match, smells, sounds, hot sun, cold snow. The walls were not quite alive, but they were at the next remove: made of crystal, played on with dimensional, super-reactionary, super-sensitive colour film and metal tape film behind glass screens, plus odorophonics and sonics.'[42]

No more coal, ashes and smoke. Houses may be heliotropic, turning towards sunshine or shade as required, and may be ventilated by 'previously filtered and sterilised air, renewed, where necessary, as in hospitals, by artificial, chemically pure air generated by dissolving aerogenic oxylith tablets, or by infusions of liquid air'.[43] For many years the lighting in houses in Kentropol has been pleasantly green in colour: 'This wonderful illumination came from phosphorescent microbes contained in tubes and globes fixed to the walls of people's rooms,'[44] and which were switched on by means of an electric spark.

The virtually immaterial relationship between the fact of pressing a button and the result obtained, whether lighting a room, setting a factory in motion, listening to the spoken newspaper, remained a source of wonder for a long time. Electricity, and later nuclear energy, make all things possible. The push-button takes a back seat; the cogs become more complicated; humans can now leave the machine to organise its own role in things. People take the articulated arms that serve them and graft them onto a body; this static trunk is then given the ability to move about; thus the robot appears. Constructed at first comically in the image of humans, they gradually become more specialised in order to carry out jobs that are disagreeable, degrading, disgusting or simply tiring. We find agricultural robots, oily and overworked, hauling giant ploughs and harrows in their whistling, steaming wake.[45] Then, in the transition to more intelligent industrial robots we approach a future that has an increasing degree of verisimilitude. As they voyage into the future, untrammelled by doubt, our illustrators may cap their visions with the perfect roundness of a sterile and aseptic dome. Everything is too clear, too simple, too perfect in this year 2000: we feel that it's time that the robots revolted, that the machines rusted, that the computers broke down; time for invaders to come and trample on the flower beds. Some authors are already feeling uneasy; they have gone off to scout around in the darker regions of the future.

23. *Variable-speed moving pavements amid the din and glare of publicity walls. 1929*

The world looked set for domination by technology. Each year that passed brought its share of novelties of every kind; a never-ending process of technical advance offered infinite possibilities of

A wo
gears and

extrapolation, but also had the effect of quickly rendering visions of the future out-of-date. There would be machines at the heart of every operation in the future, machines to fulfil every function, even the most pointless or implausible. In their variety and their occasional obscurity, the roles that would be assigned to them would match the complexity of the tasks which would be needed in an advanced society. The energy needed to drive them, or of which they would be the agents, still appeared phenomenal, and was to be matched by the wisdom of the people who would be using them. There would be little or no problem in controlling them.

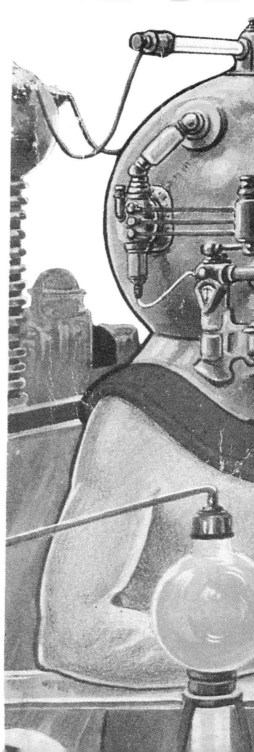

rld of

cogs

2. *The mechanised, rationalised, intensive agriculture of tomorrow. 1905*

Man invents the machine. The machine in turn creates a world in its own image, grounded in a rigorous logic, and man finds himself lost in an environment that has become gigantic, never-ending, disproportionate in scale, autonomous and self-perpetuating. Should he master it, fight it, or attempt to understand it? It is up to him to restore meaning to the world.

Sometimes, while the individual grows and flourishes in comfort, with his every need immediately satisfied, society has complex mechanisms, intelligent systems, which act as extensions of, or substitutions for, basic human functions. Other scenarios, however, depict an awesome scene, in which the power harnessed by omnipresent machines engenders a fearful respect.

Slaves of Steel. Machines are the children of both the first Industrial Revolution — that of coal and steam engines — and the second — of electricity and the internal combustion engine. For those living at the end of the nineteenth and beginning of the twentieth centuries, they represented the image of progress. Comparisons between these monsters of iron and steel and the men, horses, sweat and candles which they replaced were initially flattering. 'The novelists who devote their time to the genre of "anticipation" literature, and who amuse themselves by "imagining" what our civilisation is going to look like in two or three hundred years, represent this future world as having been revolutionised by a universal and intensive application of machinery. No more slow, laborious manual labour; everywhere human labour is replaced by machines which are marvels of activity, ingenuity and speed.'[1] Images of the future are invaded by mechanical monsters: it is impossible to depict the years and centuries to come without these metal giants. 'Pneumatic pile-drivers as big as towers, mechanical diggers with huge scoops, drilling machines capable of climbing mountains and opening up mines. From within these machines, sheltered by an armoured shell that looks like a battleship turret, men oversee the operations of dynamiting and excavation.'[2]

Often the human element is absent from these depictions. This does not imply the exclusion of humanity from the modern world; on the contrary, it remains its directing principle, its ordering force. In the final analysis, a machine represents pure labour. Mankind has

1. *Preceding double page: Machines will make it possible to penetrate the secrets of the subconscious. 1929*

3. *An automatic bill poster. 1919*

Why should our apartments not be as comfortable as certain armaments factories which are soundproofed, dust-free, and provided with air conditioning and rational lighting?

André Labarthe, 1947[5]

freed itself from labour, and life becomes wonderful: 'These simple apparatuses will provide everything that future humanity needs in terms of energy, heating and light; they will oversee the operation of its slave machines; they will also govern the seasons and the climate; earth will finally be liberated from servitude and will heat and light itself on its own account, marching before the face of the sun in the radiance of its own light.'[3]

An all-powerful mankind governs this complex of machinery, sets its pistons in motion and masters its phenomenal power. All that a human being needs to do is to shift a lever and energy bursts forth and sets in motion motors, dynamos, turbines. 'From time to time, he flicks a switch, turns the power on or off, receives orders by telephone, passes them on, and in his hand he nonchalantly holds a tiny lever capable of setting in motion a wheel which is a hundred feet in diameter and which does the work of a hundred men.'[4] Here the dominant mythology is still that of the 'push button', but now pressing the button enables you not merely to listen to the spoken newspaper of the twenty-first century, or to order a chemical meal, but to set a whole factory in motion, to light an entire city, or to drive a monstrous vehicle that is supercharged with captive energy.

The tendency towards enormity of scale means that technological uncertainties may be concealed; on the cover of a pulp illustrated by Frank R. Paul we find a giant mirror suspended in space and designed to capture solar energy and transmit it back to earth. We think of Charles Cros and his project for using similar methods to capture and concentrate the light of the sun and transmit it to the planet Mars, in an attempt

4. *Gigantic machines will replace manual labour. 1891*

to communicate with any beings living there. He took it for granted that if there were beings on Mars they would understand, and would reply. The future world, with its rationally ordered internal workings, satisfied a basic desire for order, but had no place for imagination or normal biological functioning.

The Original Function. There was no need to 'worry about a shortage of coal for our descendants. They will find as much coal as they need for their machines, their gas, and the smelting of their iron. But will people perhaps dream of other fuels than these? Who knows

if these are the most economical or the most convenient?'[6] Others would take their place: it soon became clear that electricity would be one of them, but there would also be those discovered in the twentieth century or invented for the purposes of science fiction. 'Despite the determined opposition of the big producers of atomic energy, the number of vehicles running on quintessence increased rapidly, and the combustion engine seemed set to eliminate atomic turbine and accumulator-driven motors. With quintessence, which was obtained from the fermentation and distillation of sea water, a driver could travel a thousand kilometres on half a litre of fuel.'[7] In order to fire the Tantra interstellar spacecraft, 'Pel Lynn turned the handle switching on the anameson motors. Four tall cylinders of boron nitride that could be seen through a slit in the control desk were lit up from inside. A bright green flame beat inside them with lightning speed, it flowed and whirled in four tight spirals. Up forward, in the nose of the spaceship, a strong magnetic field enveloped the motor jets, saving them from instant destruction.'[8] In the twenty-fifth century, Buck Rogers made the

acquaintance of new techniques which the world had developed during his five-hundred-year sleep: 'I visited the plants where ultrasonic vibrations were isolated from the ether and through slow processes built up into sub-electronic, electronic and atomic forms into the two great synthetic elements, ultron and inertron.'[9]

Awed by the prospect of technological progress, writers and illustrators gave their imaginations full rein in describing the world of the future, with its corridors of steel, its menacing metal labyrinths that exude a sense of contained power and are heavy with the threat to crush the poor mass of flesh and blood standing before them. It may be that the original *raison d'être* of these machines is forgotten. They are there in order to produce and to represent what, at that time, was seen as the (supposedly) triumphant march of progress. When man's efforts are supplemented by large-scale machinery, the results may be incredible: 'Machines can operate quite happily in temperatures of several hundred degrees and at pressures

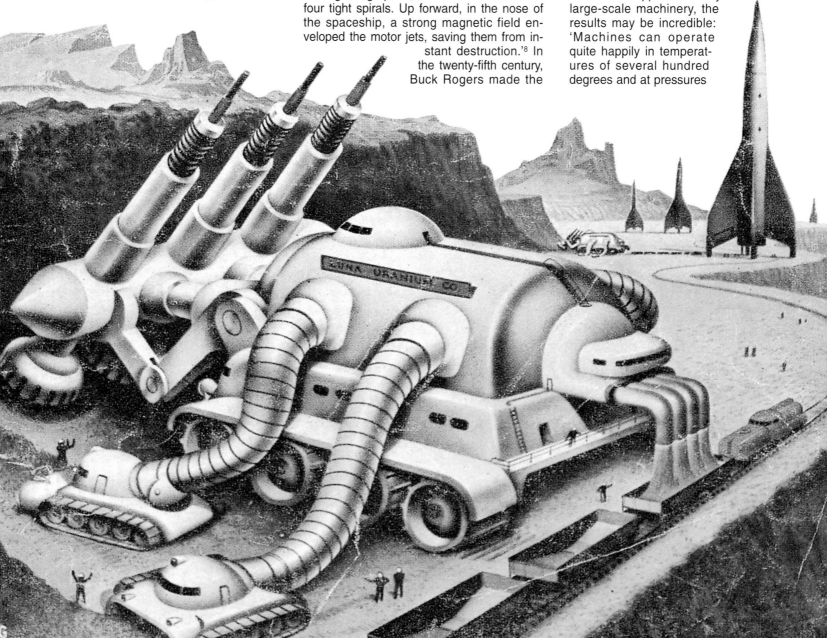

6. *Paris-London by jet-powered aero-cab. 1958*

of scores of atmospheres, and this is just what the robot moles of the near future will be doing, miles beneath our feet.'[10]

For humanity to seek, for example, to govern the power of the tides, or to capture electricity from the atmosphere, is to play at being Titans: 'It is not inconceivable that we shall be able to establish contact between clouds and special accumulators via superconducting cables; these will be raised to a suitable height by hollow spheres made of ultra-light metal and filled with a gas capable of lifting them, such as helium; here they will gather atmospheric electricity on special conducting spikes.'[11]

Elsewhere, bold, imaginative and misunderstood engineers devote themselves to dominating nature from a fortress base constructed on the Island of Beyond. There they attract hurricanes, use the power of waves to drive weaving looms, and tame a volcano in order to turn it into an enormous forge: 'The principal crater had become like an enormous cooking pot, filled with water and heated from within. An enormous metal dome covered the mouth of the crater, and it could be opened by means of large shutters if necessary, or could be

Disorder threatens our State; disorder is spreading, as is disrespect for the law. The machine must establish supreme order on this planet, it must impose, enforce and reinforce perfect and absolute order. Stanislas Lem, 1957[12]

5. *Mineral mining complex on another planet. 1952*

7. *Electricity will be captured in the clouds. 1943*

hermetically sealed by means of pressure screws. The continuous boiling of this vast mass of water supplied the steam to power the subterranean pumps and the forges located down below. All day you could hear the power hammers hammering out iron in the workshops that circled the base of the volcano.'[13] The tragic and moralistic end of the inventors of this project — latter-day descendants of Prometheus — will surprise nobody.

This optimistic and triumphant technology has its problematic side. Since one main machine makes everything run, including all the other machines, once it stops chaos ensues. People living in subterranean cities depend entirely on machinery to satisfy their needs, and have no way of dealing with a 'breakdown'.[14] When the machines fail, future humanity's dependence on them is so great that the resulting tribulations spare nobody. 'In the twentieth century, a man needed a typewriter, a telephone, a radio, a newspaper, libraries, encyclopaedias, files, yearbooks, a lawyer,

a doctor, a dentist, a chemist, a secretary . . . for all the daily actions of his life. All we need is a computer. If we want to find something, do something, record something, talk to someone . . . we push a button on our computer. Eliminate computers and everything falls apart.'[15]

Amazing Things. At first machines are represented as substitutes for man in the workplace, as a means of improving life and travel, and of making it possible to achieve new and amazing things. The ways in which they are described and illustrated are intended to give a clear, expressive and evocative image of future miracles. They symbolise power and order, speed, an appropriateness for their function, and, in some instances, a form of intelligence.

Speed dominates all the images of cars, trains, submarines and space rockets of the future. On Kentropol, an underground electric railway 'had long, bullet-shaped carriages pointed at both ends, which slid along within

a tunnel formed by huge solenoids, in other words, coils, like those of electromagnets. An alternating series of attractions and repulsions drove the shell forward down the tube in the manner of a projectile fired out of a blowgun.'[16] A Soviet vehicle of the future suggests the shape of a horizontal drop of water, 'its pointed rear end is fitted with ailerons similar to those on the tail of an aircraft. Vertical and horizontal ailerons extend the lines of the bodywork and taper to a fine edge. The perfectly smooth surface of the vehicle is devoid of door handles, bumpers and built-in windows.'[17] Ocean liners of the future, 'floating cities' of steel and glass, will sail on regardless of external conditions, and will be able to maintain phenomenal speeds through the worst weather. Similarly, stratospheric passenger aircraft will be able to travel higher and faster than ever, yet remain safe. Interplanetary space craft are inspired by the principles of ballistics: 'A freighter had a hull like a thin cigar, but surrounded by four huge fuel tanks, like giant bombs, which

8. *Left: Man will master energy of terrifying power. 1953*

9. *Right: Listening to Radio Mars. 1932*

10. *The high-speed train of the 21st century, with streamlined locomotive. 1943*

Trains like this will vie with air transport for speed and comfort.

This three-tier train is gyro-stabilised. *Amazing Stories,* 1944[22]

were jettisoned as soon as they were dry.'[18] Even astronauts adopt aerodynamic positions when they move around in space with their jet pistols.

Cross-sections and Descriptions.
Elsewhere, one sees the development of a highly rational and compartmentalised organisation of space: in the cities there are rabbit-warren tower blocks, giant factories, artificial islands, submarines, and huge transatlantic aircraft. The noted manufacturer Bréguet 'thinks that future transport aircraft will be extremely large . . . In order to increase tonnage while at the same time maintaining comfort, we will see the development of aircraft which have thick wings capable of housing passengers.'[19] Technical descriptions may be extremely precise; the 'telechromophotophonotetrascope' consists of 'a chromophotograph machine which provides the colour proof, a megagraph which enlarges it, a stenophotographic machine which gathers and records the words of the subject, assisted by a microphone which amplifies them and sends them down a telephone. This is connected to a tetrascope in order to transmit the sound and image. The various different sections of the instrument combine the sum of their efforts and transmit the product into a final receiver called a phenakistoscope, which is an acoustic lorgnette by means of which one can both see and hear.'[20] In the course of one expedition, Buck Rogers equips himself with supersensitive ultrophones with a range of eighteen miles, and 'a pair of ear discs, each a separate and self-contained receiving set. They slipped into little pockets over our ears in the fabric helmets we wore, and shut out virtually all extraneous sounds. The chest discs were likewise self-contained sending sets, strapped to the chest a few inches below the neck and actuated by the vibrations from the vocal cords through the body tissues.'[21] Machines make possible the impossible (or what was thought to be impossible).

Science has the ability to create artificial atmospheres on the surfaces of hostile planets; the icy wastes of the Arctic can be transformed into fertile fields. In this latter example, the idea is that radio wave vibrations act on the hydrogen atoms which make up the polar ice, transforming them into heavy hydrogen and at the same time releasing heat. This then enables a temperate atmosphere to be maintained in the area between two radio beams. In another instance, the extraction of thermal

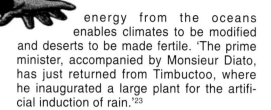

energy from the oceans enables climates to be modified and deserts to be made fertile. 'The prime minister, accompanied by Monsieur Diato, has just returned from Timbuctoo, where he inaugurated a large plant for the artificial induction of rain.'[23]

Ex Machina. In the fictional history of the future, a privileged place is reserved for the time machine. Sleep, drugs, various states of suspended animation, psychic force and accidental crossing into a time warp are all capable of providing the same result, but the time machine has a place all of its own, with many authors exploring its possibilities. After H. G. Wells, who invented it, and Jarry, the renowned pataphysician, the patent seekers have been legion. The device is simple: 'A small, simple cabin with two seats, a baggage compartment and some buttons on the control panel.' Once inside, 'I shall press a green button and everything around us will disappear. You will see a kind of haze envelope the cockpit; this is probably the field which prevents us from being affected by the passage through time.'[24] There have

The Japanese have successfully achieved a return-trip transmission of a man from Tokyo to Singapore. The fact that he suffered slight anamorphosis (a twenty-two per cent shrinkage) seems not to have been due to systemic causes, and is being viewed as an accident of transmission. *Toute la radio*, **1959**[25]

11. *Above: Graviton will finally be put to use. 1928*

12. *Amphibious aerial transatlantic liner in the 21st century. 1935*

been even simpler devices for travelling forwards through time: 'A Time Door. Time passes on each side of it, but it is separated by several thousand years . . . I don't know the exact amount. This Door will remain open for the next two hours. You can penetrate into the future simply by moving across this circle.'[26]

There are other tantalising prospects too. By the end of the twenty-ninth century, scientists will have made possible a telepathic link between two people via fibromalachite conductors. This is surpassed, however, by a superpathic separator which permits the reception of telepathic rays, their recording, and the deciphering of thought messages.[27] Science also perfects the transfer of matter: 'Molecules are transformed into energy, line by line and layer by layer. There are "contour limiters" which eliminate the time lost as a result of the scanner going beyond the limits of the object to be transmitted. As regards the problem of synchronisation, nowadays we are achieving a precision which eliminates the risk of deformation. Disintegration and reintegration no longer pose problems.'[28] Modern man is a new Pygmalion, flirting with magic in order to bring inert objects to life. He becomes the brother of Faust, and can no longer die. Once he abandons his mortal flesh, he achieves total efficiency and immortality: 'Millions of years earlier, the Zoromes had renounced their bodies of flesh and blood and had invented machines, or robots, which did not know death and which were reparable and interchangeable.'[29]

Portable Pipe Dreams. There are machines for every purpose: all one needs to do is invent them and build them. And in the future a large number have already been patented: to annihilate enemies, be they brothers or foreigners; to correspond with beings of whose existence one cannot even be sure, let alone of their ways of thinking; to probe for distant worlds; to render hostile environments suitable for life; and to be able to farm heavily polluted land. An encounter between two spacecraft in the Crab Nebula provokes a dramatic situation which has to be resolved by making contact; the problem is that one side uses sound to communicate, and the other uses short waves.[30]

Machines collect, analyse and retransmit essential information: 'Erg Noor decided to study the planet with the help of bomb-stations. They sent out a physical research robot and the automatic recorder reported on an astonishing quantity of free oxygen in an atmosphere of neon and nitrogen, the presence of water vapour and a temperature of 12° C.'[31] Occasionally — often, in fact — people's lives become dependent on their machines, and it takes just one breakdown for the situation to appear in all its horror: 'Without the electronic calculator, we are done for. It is impossible to calculate the orbit which will enable us to return to Earth. It would take an army of mathematicians weeks to work it out.'[32]

The world is reorganised according to objective criteria. Nothing is impossible if one has the means to achieve it. The machine becomes the symbol of human intervention into nature. For example, one can modify the climate of the planet by 'suspending' artificial suns over the polar regions. 'The level of the oceans was raised by seven metres, the cold fronts receded sharply and the ring of trade winds that had dried up the deserts on the outskirts of the tropic zone became much weaker. Hurricanes and, in general, stormy weather, ceased almost completely.'[33] The enormity of mechanical power is akin in the collective imagination to the phenomenal distances involved in the transmission of sound and images. 'Man will finally emerge from this prisoner's life, this life of a bird in a cage; he will communicate with other worlds, with his brothers in space!'[34]

The infinitely large and the infinitesimally small. Machines enable things to be enlarged, reduced and multiplied at will. It even becomes possible to send a miniaturised submarine into the body of a scientist, with a team of surgeons on board charged with the task of saving his brain — and the information which it contains — from irreversible damage due to a life-threatening blood clot.

A Hellish Logic. Once the world has been opened to the rule of machines, life follows a particular course. 'Capital assets, intellect and human labour power will be organised along these lines, and each field will be organised as a machine factory, put together like the set for a fantastical stage show, or rather as a laboratory.'[35] Pragmatic and positivist, the nineteenth century gave rise to visions of the future that were based on a predominance of mechanisation and ideas of material progress. Such visions were to prevail over a long period, even

13. *The Mother-machine. 1920*

though voices were raised to highlight their drawbacks. It was to take the major social, political and ecological disasters of the twentieth century for people's eyes to be opened and for the movement to be reversed, at least partially.

In this future world, there is no room for doubt. The machine, as mythical as some metal Sphinx, reverses the classical Sphinx scenario: the machine brings answers (youth, wealth, power and authority), but it is deaf to questions. And if imbalances are created, there is still a chance of eradicating them, even within the most inhuman of scenarios. The machine, having been created by man, goes on to generate its own world and its self-perpetuating logic. In one instance, rebel vessels return to the wild and launch raids against civilisation and its supply-base fortresses.[36] Machines arrive from elsewhere and show terrestrial artefacts the path to freedom: 'A sewing machine, having become aware of its true identity and of the place it occupied in the universe, this morning showed its independence by taking a walk through the streets of this allegedly free town. . . .'[37]

Reproduction Code. The illustrations bring out the process of mechanical duplication thanks to a mirror effect which produces an infinite replication of detail: transmission belts, electric cables, solar panels, arches, multi-level bridges, and buildings that are reproduced a hundred times over. Hives, pigeonholes, cells, compartments: the physical concepts of mass confinement takes on a mental or psychic dimension. In these nightmare visions of a mechanised future, people are identical, virtually man-machines, or asexual clones, wandering mindlessly in the bowels of great factory cities.

In space one may encounter an artificial moon, the core of which is a complicated system of machinery. With its self-perpetuating logic, the mechanicist world inhabits a kind of closed circuit. One has only to think of nuclear energy today, feeding on its own processed waste in supergenerators, and

we have a concrete exemplification of Ouriboros, the serpent eating its own tail — the symbol of eternity. 'Life was marvellous on the planet, because not only did the king decree that everything that existed previously was to be improved by cybernetics, but he also legislated for a new order. This led to the kingdom producing cybercrayfish and buzzing cyberwasps, and even cyberflies which, when they began to proliferate, were caught by mechanical spiders.'[38] Once created, machines do not stop; they continue working even after his death or his disappearance — on Mars, in phantom spacecraft, in New Chicago, where everything functions by means of a practically inexhaustible intra-atomic energy. When the Gismo, a universal reproducer, was invented, all values relating to work and, effort were revolutionised. It was the start not of a new Golden Age, but of an age of slavery overseen by harsh and greedy spirits.[39] Clarke imagines a similar 'universal matter duplicator', which would comprise a memory, a data storage bank and an organiser. However, he prefers

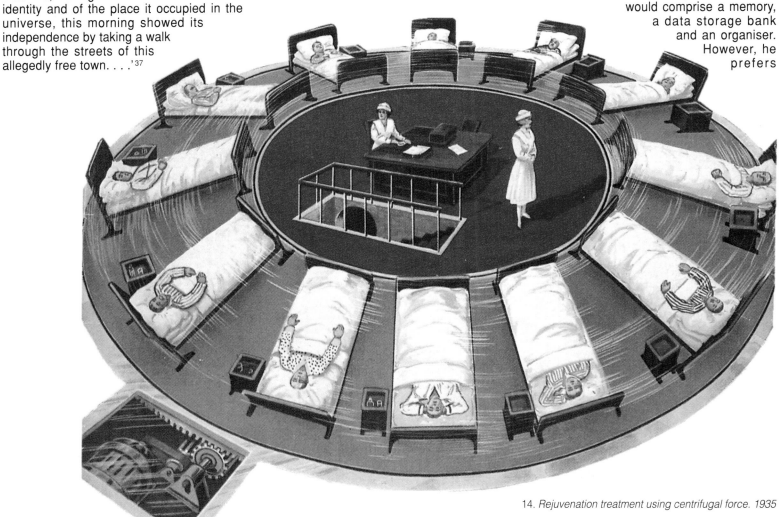

14. *Rejuvenation treatment using centrifugal force. 1935*

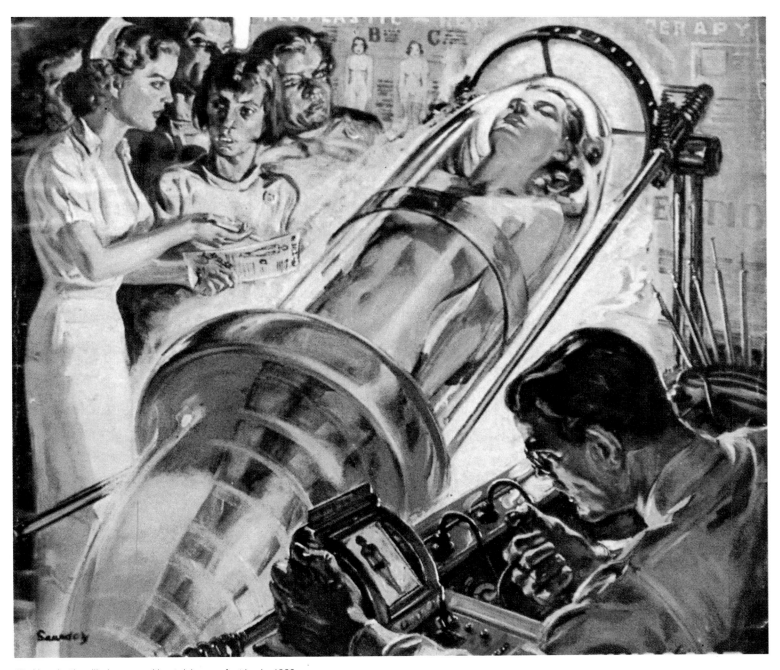

15. *Neoplastic will give you, without risk, a perfect body. 1939*

One day we may be able to enter into temporary unions with any sufficiently sophisticated machines, thus being able not merely to control but to become a spaceship or a submarine or a TV network. Arthur C. Clarke, 1962[40]

16. *Robots will be built by robots. 1950*

to project it into a more distant future, for fear that civilisation may sink into hedonism and then boredom. Confrontation with the machine world may also have an inhuman side: when the perfect drawing machine is delivered to the studio where he works, the draughtsman who has been supplanted is driven to suicide.[41]

The Machine-World. The most characteristic image of the machine-world is the giant computer, distant descendant of ENIAC (Electronic Numerical Integrator and Computer), the first true computer, built in 1946. The existence of huge computers necessarily engenders a highly hierarchical and centralised structure within a given company, country or planet. The element of giganticism extends from the instrument, originally little more than a highly developed hand, to the entity which controls it, and with thousands of others: the central computer.

Thus the Brain of the US Robots in a certain sense 'manages' the enterprise, because no decision can be taken without first consulting it. The possibility of human control over details has been abandoned in the face of the volume and specialisation

of information required. Some computers may extend beyond the framework of even the largest of companies, and become virtual cities unto themselves. The Multivac computer complex extends over a whole region of America; its giant memory stores information relating to every kind of human problem. It is at once oracle and doctor, psychiatrist and judge, policeman and nanny. In the end the Multivac computer can no longer bear being loaded with all of humanity's problems, and makes a bid to free itself: 'It wants to die.'[42] At the end of Boulevard Alpha-Ralpha, which has been abandoned for centuries, Abba-Dingo has the key to human life: 'If we have no God, at least we have a machine. It is the only thing in the world, or outside the world, which the instruments do not understand. Maybe it predicts the future. Maybe it's an anti-machine. At any rate, it's certain that its roots lie in another epoch.'[43] A Tibetan monastery uses a computer to list the 'nine billion names of God'. When the operation is complete, the stars go out one by one and the machine becomes God.[44]

Human brains are sometimes separated from their human shells and absorbed into machines. They are seen both as imprisoned spirits, and as pure intelligence, stripped of emotion and personality. The symbiosis between machine and brain is developed for the piloting of space vessels. Some writers envisage the brain of a human being transferred into a metal humanoid's body when the original body is destroyed by sickness, old age or accident.

Cybernetics is treated pessimistically in the depiction of a society where hatred for past wars drives people to resort to Immob: limbs are 'shortened' and replaced by classic prostheses, or others which may be adapted to particular

17. *Specialised robots will assist humans in mining other planets. 1929*

functions. 'All these amps were vol-amps, he knew that too. It was voluntary . . . What had happened to Theo's arms? He had cut them off voluntarily.'[45]

Robots and Co. Robots too are one of the symbols of the future. Frankenstein's creature still lay in the realm of fantasy, but with his 'future Eve' Villiers imagines an ideal woman, an automaton with the capacity for speech, a hypnotic soul, whose gentle movements are powered by electricity. Since man is not able to model clay and breathe life into it, he calls on machinery to create a stand-in for himself. But it will be an inferior being, which at first will be devoid of consciousness, operating only according to a programme; by definition it can be controlled, and it works at its master's command. What we have here is the ancient dialectic of master and slave.

The first functional robots are brothers of the automatons: they replace man, and serve him. They were designed to do everything that people found painful, boring or disgusting. Mechanical workers created in imitation of human beings, Rossum Universal Robots were androids — organic, humanoid creations. 'The android was

created to take the place of the slaves of antiquity, to do the world's donkey work and to leave humanity with the freedom to devote itself to higher works, to spiritual speculation, and to mental and physical recreation.'[46]

Two types (mechanical and biological) coexist. Among the various specialist robots one finds nurse robots and doctor robots. Robots may also function as 'shields', in order to shelter humanity from danger. They will serve as guinea pigs on journeys into space: 'These automatons are indispensable, because the shell is not designed for living beings such as ourselves to live on board.'[47] They will fight wars while humanity hides away in antinuclear bunkers. They will be at the forefront in situations of danger: in space, a mechanical robot drills an opening which is going to mean its certain destruction: 'A stream of extraordinarily bright, rainbow-coloured fire burst out of the hole, and flew off at a tangent from the spiral protruberance. This, and the fact that the blue metal melted and immediately closed the hole that had been cut, saved the unfortunate explorers. Nothing remained of the mighty robot but a mass of molten metal with two short metal legs sticking pitifully out of it.'[48]

18. *Above: Man and robot united on the road to technological progress. 1953*

19. *Right: Encounter between a nice robot and a stupid machine. 1953*

20. *Facing page: An android of rare perfection. 1954*

21. *The skill of hyper-specialised robots will exceed that of humans. 1939*

The Laws. The slave characteristics attributed to the first robots went hand in hand with a threat of revolt. This was a classic theme in the early stories, but was later abandoned, because robots cannot revolt; the robot is conceived in such a way that it must always obey and respect the moral imperatives of the three basic laws of robotics, as formulated by the eminent Professor Asimov. Robots are portrayed as ideal types of the models which they are intended to replace: shoe salesmen, extractors of radioactive waste, detectives, lawyers, replacement wives and children. In cases where robots are perfect replicas, the humans who meet them inevitably feel a sense of embarrassment or vague danger. On occasion they also express a frank hostility, or a latent guilt:"'Certainly, sir, and I see that you like a joke," acquiesced the electronically affable barman.'[49] Humanity's arrogance and sense of superiority in the face of simple robots change to fear when confronted with robots that are too perfect and too intelligent. The same reflexes arise in the face of very sophisticated machines: the fear of unemployment, and an anguished questioning of the intrinsic value of the individual. The robot itself may give the answer. The difference of conception between a positronic brain and a biological brain reveals the value of human reasoning, which has the capacity to be illogical if necessary. To be fallible is at once both a danger and a strength for humans.

Exegesis. The evolution of robots relates to their increasing specialisation. If they take on human form, it is not by reason of the excessive anthropocentrism or narcissism of their designers, but for reasons of efficiency and productivity. However, sophisticated robots built on the basis of human values may find themselves faced with a dilemma which drives them mad, blows their circuits, or leads them to become hysterical like humans. We meet robots who may be deviant, childish, scatterbrained or failures in life. The three laws of robotics are not designed to raise dilemmas, or to give rise to interpretations. So writers have to imagine paradoxical situations which threaten the stability of the three laws, and render the robots psychologically fragile. In order to sort out programming problems and resolve conflicts between robots, companies may call on the services of robot psychologists.

If robots are tinkered with they become capable of amazing things. The creators of Helen, a sexed robot, provide her with a capacity for emotion; she will end up by spending her life with one of them. 'A perfect female model. The plastic and rubberite used for the face had the required flexibility to express emotions, and everything was there, including tear glands and taste buds.

Everything was ready to simulate human actions, from simply breathing to tearing one's hair out.'[50] A telepathic robot tells lies in order not to hurt the feelings of the humans with whom it associates. Among the prototypes, we also have an insatiable do-it-yourself robot which builds other specialist robots.

In cases where humanity becomes extinct, robots may end up becoming the final repositories of human morality, history and values; occasionally memories become confused and end up being turned into legends. Men are known by robots as 'websters', from the name of one of the families that has come down through history.[51]

Cyborgs (symbiotic beings which are both man and machine) are feared. They are perceived as an exogenous danger; they are a source of hurt pride for humanity, because they are a blow to man's integrity and the mental image of what it is that constitutes man (body, brain, spirit). Rejection of transplantations is more psychological than physical, but: 'If we cannot prevent our bodies from disintegrating, we may replace them while there is yet time. The replacement need not be another body of flesh and blood; it could be a machine, and this may represent the next stage in evolution.'[52]

22. The inventor will no longer understand his own machine. 1941

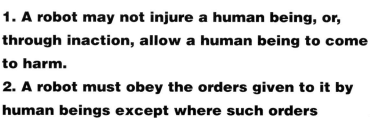

1. A robot may not injure a human being, or, through inaction, allow a human being to come to harm.

2. A robot must obey the orders given to it by human beings except where such orders would conflict with the First Law.

3. A robot must protect its own existence as long as such protection does not conflict with the First or Second Law.

Isaac Asimov, 1942[53]

23. A deviant robot. 1930

75

The ge the future

Most prophecies glorified what was effectively the only possible setting of this new technophile universe: the city. Over entire continents we find nothing but cities; the entire human race will end up living in a scattering of colossal cities, which will provide shelter for the survivors of devastated lands or of lands which have been simply abandoned. In these cities everything will necessarily move very fast and will be very noisy. They will grow larger and larger, and human beings will aggregate like coral. We shall find refuges being built for an overpopulated humanity, taking New York as their model, but on a vaster scale, and all perfectly clean. Other kinds of cities will also arise, perhaps built in one single block, or extending horizontally and endlessly. Eventually, they will be built underground and will no longer even be given names.

ometry of

The city of the future is a city of wonders. It has its roots in the richest soil imaginable: the glorious and unattainable schemes that have been dreamed up by imagination, faith and Utopianism over the years. With the passing of Plato's ideal city and the heavenly city of Jerusalem, cities designed by men on the basis of an idea give way to types of architecture which can be catalysers of inventions, ideas and projects for the future. The organisation of society, the philosophy which presides over its destiny, and the place reserved for each individual — all this will be reflected in the projected cities of the future.

Since the schemes of writers and illustrators are not conceived for realisation, even in theoretical terms, they are free to plunder, pervert, corrupt and even anticipate the visions of architects and urbanists as the fancy takes them. However, for many of them the city of the future existed already. It was there, before their eyes, symbolised by New York or Chicago — a frenzy of buildings which evinced alternate reactions of enthusiasm and repulsion. The cities portrayed in the pages of this book distinguish themselves from pure architecture or from life-size

1. *Preceding page: Aerial station with railway connection. 1916*

2. *Left: The Eiffel Tower, symbol of bygone days, is eclipsed by gigantic modern buildings. 1932*

Gigantic globes of cool white light shamed the pale sunbeams that filtered down through the girders and wires. Here and there a gossamer suspension bridge dotted with foot passengers flung across the chasm and the air was webbed with slender cables. H. G. Wells, 1899 [1]

prototypes in two principal respects: first, to describe them it is necessary to use superlatives which, when taken together, go beyond any possible drawing-board scenario; second, it is intrinsically impossible that they will ever exist in real life, a fact which automatically consigns them to the realm with which we are concerned in this book — that of the idealised future.

Buzzing Aerocabs. As a focus of human intercourse, the city comes across as the most busy and bustling phenomenon of the future. This is a city rooted in history, a continuum within which the medieval city is succeeded by the Baroque city, and then the modern city, which itself gives way to the city of the future. But this latter will have its own archaeology, whether real or invented, and writers and illustrators have felt the need to provide familiar reference points. The city may be immense and never-ending, but in its plunging perspectives, amid the tangle of aerial bridges, one still detects familiar monuments — in the case of Paris, the Opéra, the Arc de Triomphe, Notre-Dame and the Eiffel Tower; in London, St Paul's Cathedral and the Tower of London . . . Elsewhere, even if years or even centuries separate the reader from the city in question, we are still dealing with one or other of the capitals of the Western world; on occasion they change name and become Nu-Yok, New London or New Chicago.

Moving pavements, transparent roads, multi-level circulation of traffic — these are some of the options envisaged in order to deal with the problems of the city of the future, which are rather more dramatic than those of broken paving stones and inconsiderate drivers. Seen from above, they have long, uninterrupted streams of traffic moving down their broad avenues like armies of small beetles. In a complex web of proliferating interconnections, the city is organic and open, and seems to develop with no apparent order or overall directing schema. Light aircraft clutter the skies; the overhead railway, with its iron trelliswork arches, crosses paths with the underground railway at strategic points in the city. Suspension bridges serve as interconnections between tower blocks, giving a spider-like poetry to the whole.

'Tall stone-built blocks are linked to each other at each level by bold arching bridges, and a complex network of transport routes gives the whole an appearance of fifty cities one on top of the other, swarming with

3. Aerial bridges link the skyscrapers which pack the Paris skies. 1910

crowds of moving people.'[2] These visions derive principally from the iron and steel architecture characteristic of the nineteenth century, which gave us Paxton's Crystal Palace and Baltard's Les Halles, and which is best symbolised in the lacework patterning of the Eiffel Tower. The bubbling up and bursting forth of new forms, new sources of energy, and novel modes of transport invade those old cities which still permit themselves to grow in anarchic fashion. Present-day conditions are transposed into the future: we hear of aerial traffic jams, for instance. The city of the future is no longer a city of right angles. There are more hissing trains billowing smoke, and buzzing aeroplanes with vibrating wings, than there are cars stuck in traffic jams. Sometimes, however, cars not only invade the multi-level streets — they may even climb up the side of tower blocks, up snaking roads which look like mule tracks going up a mountain. Platforms are constructed on the tops of buildings for flying vehicles to land on.

However, regulatory ideas do arise: 'Twelve ring roads, more or less equally spaced, divide the city into concentric zones.

4. Left: Aeroplanes will land on the tops of towers. 1943

5. Below: The idealised urbanism of the city of the future. 1920

6. Right: A symbiosis of fortifications and metallic architecture for an imaginary city. 1890

To right and left there was a series of endless pavements, each of which travelled at seven miles an hour faster than the pavement to its left, so that one could move from one pavement to another until one reached the outer pavement, which was the fastest, and one could cross the whole city like this. H. G. Wells, 1899 [3]

From the outer ring, a number of radials converge on the centre, but without reaching it, since they stop at the fifth zone. This gives plenty of possibilities of communication between the various points of the outer lines. The spaces enclosed within the strands of this vast network are served by electric vehicles which cut across it in all directions.'[4] Some writers describe holiday resorts and a means of escaping from the hurly-burly; but perhaps it's already too late, for nature has become silent. Our authors describe a process of inevitable evolution, of how 'life in households was steadily supplanted by life in

7. *Left: In 2889, a row of identical towers will house the population of an entire town. 1933*

8. *Below: An artificial island containing a maritime port, airport, factory and international hotel. 1935*

9. *Right: Above the subterranean tunnels and the elevated streets, the future city will rise up, gigantic, made up of buildings which are themselves small towns. 1939*

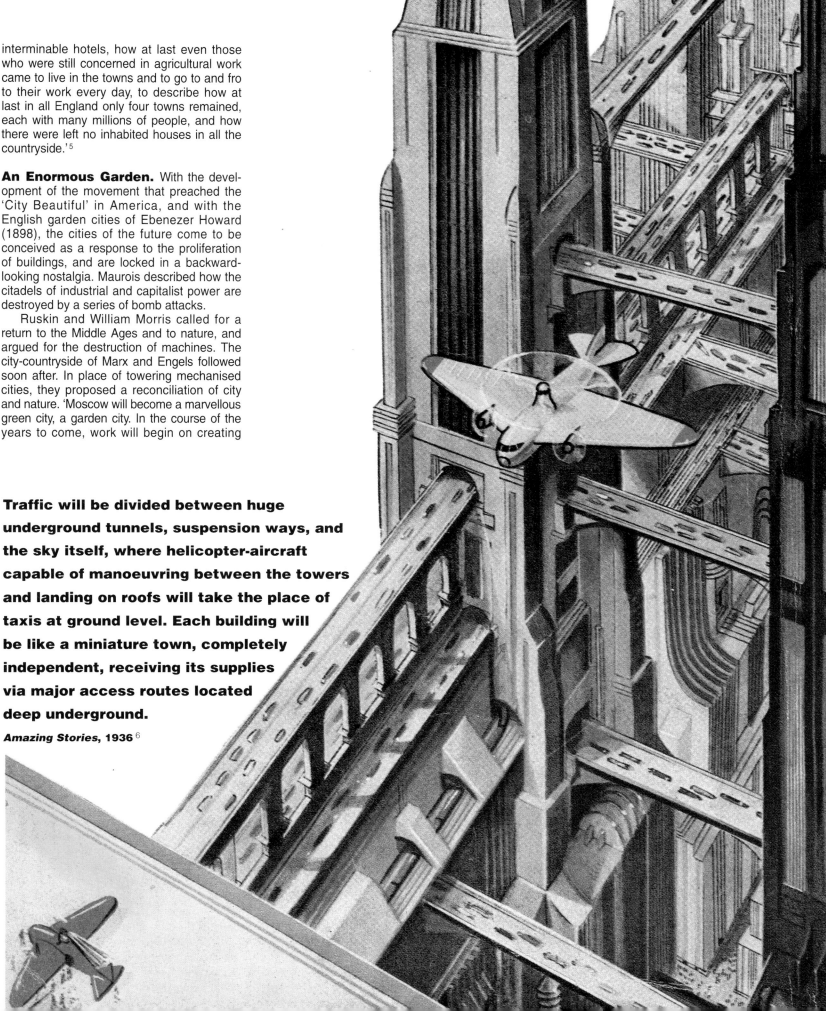

interminable hotels, how at last even those who were still concerned in agricultural work came to live in the towns and to go to and fro to their work every day, to describe how at last in all England only four towns remained, each with many millions of people, and how there were left no inhabited houses in all the countryside.'[5]

An Enormous Garden. With the development of the movement that preached the 'City Beautiful' in America, and with the English garden cities of Ebenezer Howard (1898), the cities of the future come to be conceived as a response to the proliferation of buildings, and are locked in a backward-looking nostalgia. Maurois described how the citadels of industrial and capitalist power are destroyed by a series of bomb attacks.

Ruskin and William Morris called for a return to the Middle Ages and to nature, and argued for the destruction of machines. The city-countryside of Marx and Engels followed soon after. In place of towering mechanised cities, they proposed a reconciliation of city and nature. 'Moscow will become a marvellous green city, a garden city. In the course of the years to come, work will begin on creating

Traffic will be divided between huge underground tunnels, suspension ways, and the sky itself, where helicopter-aircraft capable of manoeuvring between the towers and landing on roofs will take the place of taxis at ground level. Each building will be like a miniature town, completely independent, receiving its supplies via major access routes located deep underground.

Amazing Stories, 1936 [6]

green belts and irrigating the south-west territory. Here, where the majestic edifice of the Pantheon will be constructed, as a tomb for the best sons and daughters of our people, a colossal forest park will be created. The muddy river Sietun will become a necklace of blue lakes. Mirror-like lakes will gleam in place of today's gulleys.'[7] Another model — this time 'naturalist' — appeared in 1934: Frank Lloyd Wright's Broadacre City project, a scheme for an extended city in which dispersed apartment blocks rise from the midst of trees, and where terrestrial communications networks are highly developed, complemented by personal helicopters. This is the kind of living environment enjoyed by the Spacers, the aristocrats of the future, who shun contact with Earthians (who are seen as bearers of contagious germs), and who protect themselves behind an impenetrable barrier: in Spacetown, 'every family has its own house, with a dome roof over it, and under the dome they have land.'[8]

One also finds descriptions of the highly regulated life imposed by urban conditions as denounced by the counter-Utopians: 'They were flying over the six-kilometre zone of parkland that separated Central London from its first ring of satellite suburbs. The green was maggoty with foreshortened life. Forests of centrifugal Bumble-puppy towers gleamed between the trees. Near Shepherd's Bush two thousand BetaMinus mixed couples were playing Riemann-surface tennis.'[9]

10. *Elevated streets and an aerial transport network might alleviate the extreme density of cities in the 21st century. 1928*

This is the city of the twenty-first century, a colossus of metal, plastic and unbreakable glass. A city that has reached its highest point of culture, a city of science, of atomic power and of voyages into space. *Amazing Stories,* **1942**[10]

Cement, Steel and Clouds. However, in the 1930s the city of the future was already there, in the shape of Manhattan Island, an offshoot of the gigantic city which had given birth to such a wealth of stories and images. As early as 1844, Ralph Waldo Emerson, commenting on its symbolic value, concluded: 'America is the country of the future.' The first skyscraper in New York was built in 1902, on the corner of Fifth Avenue and 23rd Street, and was soon joined by other iron, steel and concrete giants. This surging growth was so rapid that links with the past were eradicated, and the city of 'before' was pushed back to the periphery of this glorious, aggressive excrescence. Cities of the future would, for a long time, use New York almost unanimously as their model, until the time when another model imposed itself. What we see reproduced in the projection of future cities is the Rockefeller Centre raised to a factor of ten. The real city and the invented city interpenetrate, with the latter modifying the urban fabric inherited from the former and trying to provide answers to the questions raised by the gigantic scale, the congestion and the enormous growth predicted for future years. The new city is young and can no longer allow itself to grow unchecked. 'The increase in traffic jams due to the vast scale of buildings leads one to think that it will be necessary for traffic to be separated onto several levels. Whatever one does to improve traffic-flow, it seems that we are powerless to check its incessant growth. Many experts believe that the only suitable solution would be in the third dimension. For example, pedestrians may be encouraged to circulate on separate raised walkways above the traffic, which itself may circulate above railways.'[11] The multi-level circulation of traffic proposed by the architect Hugh Ferriss repeatedly crops up in the cities portrayed in pulp magazines. The massive verticality of the mechanical concrete city is tunnelled through by traffic routes which pass from one side of a building to the other, violating the buildings but still leaving them dominant.

11. The Metropolis of Tomorrow
*by the architect Hugh Ferriss,
or the Manhattan-style city as
symbol of modernity. 1929*

When these vast problems of transportation became too critical to be capable of regulation by political solutions, the local communities entrusted them to 'semi-public Port, Bridge and Highway Authorities: huge capital-investment ventures modelled upon the Port of New York Authority, which had shown its ability to build and/or run such huge operations as the Holland and Lincoln Tunnels, the George Washington Bridge, Teterboro, La Guardia, Idlewild and Newark airports, and many lesser facilities.'[12]

The moral significance of the American city, representing as it does hard work, daring and prosperity, explains its persistence as a model for cities of the future, particularly in its verticality and its dynamic geometry: 'In the future, with the evolution of cities, New Yorkers really will live in the sky. There will be aerial walkways in parks, and high-level golf courses. Instead of going to the country, people will go "up" to get their fresh air. Terraces on the top of towers in the residential areas will mean that children will be able to play outdoors again. The inhabitants will spend a lot of time out in the open. There will be aviation hangars, and people will use aeroplanes in the same way that today they use their cars.'[13]

Cubic Zoning. Imagination and theoretical thinking tend to become distanced from the use of reality as a model. What is being redesigned for tomorrow's world is a city that is no

12. *Nomadic space-cities escaping earth's gravitational pull. 1929*

longer historic, but instead is preconceived and responds to a pre-existing vision. The temptation to Utopianism gives rise to an *a priori* city, which is perfectly geometrical, perhaps star-shaped or radial, and is inherited from the ideal city of the Renaissance. The city of the future is reshaped along a web-shaped or chequer-patterned grid. In instances where it embodies a philosophy of progress, it has built-in systems of constraint and repression. The freedoms accorded to its citizens have the result of 'naturally grouping the inhabitants according to their lifestyles. Thus, without anyone having consciously planned it, there are some streets which are inhabited only by quiet, married couples, and where everybody is in bed by nine o'clock. In other streets, houses are occupied by single people, noisily engaged in the pursuit of pleasure; sometimes they spend whole nights singing and drinking without the neighbours daring to complain, because all the neighbours will have been equally noisy in their time.'[14]

A strict division of labour, function and location echoes the rule of reason governing the Platonic city, with the threefold division of its inhabitants into philosophers, guardians and producers. Different divisions have been

13. *Above: Atomic city of the future, enclosed within a dome, regimented, devoid of natural light. 1952*

14. *Right: More than 83% of households will have a private aeroplane and all buildings will be designed to accommodate them. 1931*

Through the thick glass walls of the buildings he saw thousands of workers toiling relentlessly in rooms that were completely sterile, bathed in the ultraviolet rays of sunlight which the glass filtered through.

Wallace G. West, 1929[15]

envisaged, however, such as work, administration and home, or work, leisure and sleep. Tony Garnier's Cité Industrielle (1901) featured the basic elements, such as a grid layout, zoning (residential areas, industry, offices), the use of concrete, flat roofs, and a generous provision of parks. 'The appearance of the countryside was quite different from the countryside that I knew. All the roads had houses along them; innumerable canals traced their silvery tracks across the fields.'[16] The breakthrough occasioned in the last century by Darwinism and the Industrial Revolution enabled a transition from a cyclical vision to a vision of history that was 'progressive' and evolutive. This meant that it was no longer really possible for modern thinkers to work to a notion of the perfect Model City. 'The Ministry of Truth contained, it was said, three thousand rooms above ground level, and corresponding ramifications below. Scattered about London there were just three other buildings of similar appearance and size. So completely did they dwarf the surrounding architecture that from the roof of Victory Mansions you could see all four of them simultaneously. They were the homes of the four Ministries between which the entire apparatus of government was divided.'[17]

16. Between New York and New Jersey, 20-lane bridges will draw together the individual solitude of thousands of people. 1929

15. Floating city in the middle of the ocean. 1928

If you're born in a cubicle and grow up in a corridor, and work in a cell, and vacation in a crowded sun-room, then coming up into the open with nothing but sky over you might just give you a nervous breakdown. Isaac Asimov, 1951[18]

17. *On the surface of the globe there will be nothing but megapolises linked by high-speed transport. 1934*

You have never seen the sun. Or rain, or snow, or the night-time stars.

The towns are covered by huge domes of protective rays which block out the sky.

It's always daytime in the towns. Francis Flagg, 1932 [19]

Space. In these theoretical cities, aesthetics takes precedence over habitability. Some cities seem entirely alive and habitable, albeit standardised, while others fit purely ideological criteria. A space thus conceptualised could not be inhabited by real human beings. 'They travelled down the long rectilinear boulevards at a crazy speed, flanked by skyscrapers that glittered with a strange beauty. Everything was so dazzlingly clean that it made you feel kind of dizzy.'[20]

The norm is uniformisation. Le Corbusier shattered the traditional structure of the city by replacing it with parallelepipeds that were laid out in green surroundings, each living unit turned inwards upon itself, so as to form an independent and autonomous microcosm. The Cité Radieuse embodies the principles of the phalanstery, and applies them in an urban living space which is unitary, efficient and atomised. The future city's functionalism derives from an intellectual rather than a biological scheme of the city, that is, from a rational structuring of living space.

The separation of functions which defines the internal workings of a given urban space may extend to the country as a whole. 'She knew vaguely how the industrial towns were governed. In each one there was a garrison of Pinks, and of Scholars, a class of functionaries halfway between Pinks and Purples, who ran the factories and operated as engineers. None of them lived in the industrial towns. They had their houses miles away, in the Flower-Cities, and they travelled to work by air.'[21] In his study of the 'cybernetic city', Nicolas Schöffer advocates a separation between the functional and residential parts of the city, arguing that the values of relaxation and population deconcentration will be favoured by horizontality, while those of contact and population concentration will be stimulated by verticality. In other cities the division of urban space is governed by the existence of enemy castes: 'One of these days, we the Flat-Heads and you Pointy-Heads are going to call a truce, and then we should head up there and sort out the Folks at the Old Windmills,' she shouted, in a tense, emotional voice. 'Let's go and burn their houses down — that'll teach them not to think themselves better than us.'[22]

The lethal perfection of a town planning based on the rigid alignment of streets, the endless reproduction of identical tower

18. *Traffic control at city road junctions. 1934*

blocks, and the omnipresence of transparent glass suggests the psychological crushing of the individual. The individual becomes lost in this scenario of endless horizons and plunging verticalities. 'Down below, people were turning, bending and getting up, in time, with rapid rhythmic gestures, as if they had been Taylorised. They worked as if they were the pistons of some enormous machine. Blue flames flared from tubes that they held in their hands. They were using these flames to cut and weld blocks of glass. Great transparent monsters made of glass moved slowly down rails that were also made of glass. These were the cranes.'[23]

Under the Dome. The questions raised by problems — both real (overpopulation, the clogging of the metropolis) and conjectured — can give rise to alternative forms of cities. The vertical Manhattan model, which has exercised such a power over visions of the future, has sometimes consciously been avoided — the ritual murder of the mother city. The model is done away with. 'Towns will be supplied with conditioned air, abandoning the old

19. *The aggressive splendour of Nu-Yok in the hands of the Mongols. 1934*

system of air conditioning in individual buildings and shifting to plastic domes which will cover the whole city — although some experts foresee the use of magnetic fields. Even in the countryside, the air will be controlled.'[24] The visitor notices how 'It was as though the reverie of some city-planning visionary had been peeled from a drawing board, blown up, and pasted life-size over the countryside.'[25] The city may be too

perfect, too clean, too straight-edged, but it is decidedly 'futurist'. And in cases like this, the use of familiar names has an opposite effect, aggressively accentuating the break with a past which is somehow mocked by the use of the term 'New': New Jamestown, New Tolstoygrad, New Singapore, New Saigon, New Surabaya. 'They will have flung great arches and domes of glass above the wider spaces of the town, the slender beauty of the perfect metal-work far overhead will be softened to a fairy-like insubstantiality by the mild London air. It will be the London air we know, clear of filth and all impurity, the same air that gives our October days their unspeakable clarity and makes every London twilight mysteriously beautiful.'[26] It may be that the original city disappeared, in the wake of a conflict, a war or a nuclear explosion. On the other hand, the writer and the illustrator may decide deliberately to create a place located outside familiar, habitual reference points, even without some previous disaster, and without explaining the reason for the break; here the purpose is simply to make it radically different and distanced as much as possible from reality.

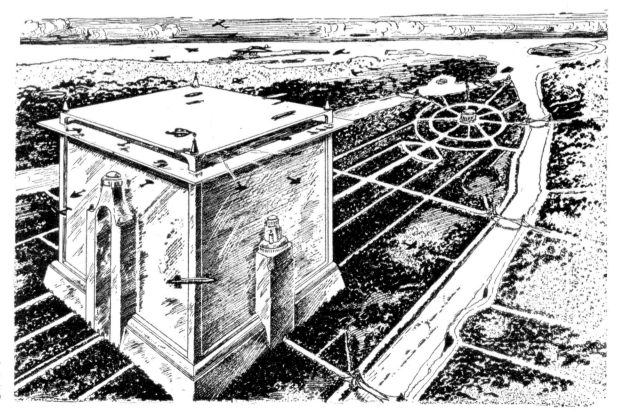

20. *On Manhattan Island, 80 million people will live on 800 floors in a gigantic cubic city three kilometres wide and high. 1930*

21. Metropolis, *the future as seen by Fritz Lang. 1926*

Cities beneath domes, huge towers with independent lives of their own, systems of machinery which crush the non-conformist individual, cities built as bridges . . . There are many, many models, but they all depict spaces that are closed. The cities of the dominant Han 'were entirely enclosed, with splendid arrangements for ventilation and heating. These arrangements of course were equally adequate in their airships. The Hans, indeed, had quite a distaste for unshaded daylight, since their lighting apparatus diffused a controlled amount of ultraviolet rays, making the unmodified sunlight unnecessary for health, and undesirable for comfort.'[27]

Concentration, efficiency and productivity do not necessarily succeed in resolving the problems caused by overpopulation. The drop in people's standard of living means that there is not enough food to feed an overpopulated planet, so the only thing that can save humanity from disaster is effective organisation. Everything that was small (artisan production, small industry, villages, small towns . . .) disappears. In its place comes gigantism, a concentration of production and of human living space.

22. *In America, enormous city-bridges will be built. 1929*

Towns become shut in on themselves: very dependent, very fragile, but held together by an artificial cement — the necessity of people living in 'hives housing great swarms of humanity'. New York grew to extend across an area of 3,000 square kilometres, with twenty million inhabitants; in the whole world there remain only eight hundred cities, of approximately ten million inhabitants each. 'Each City became a semi-autonomous unit, economically all but self-sufficient. It could roof itself in, gird itself about, burrow itself under. It became a steel cave, a tremendous, self-contained cave of steel and concrete.'[28]

On the one hand, cities wall themselves in, and on the other there is open desert, a frightening no-man's-land; people may create myths about it, or it may even be forgotten. 'The car passed between two 800-metre high structures, and suddenly found itself in the middle of the countryside. There were no suburbs, not even villages. The city came to an abrupt stop; it was now behind them, glittering like a pile of diamonds.'[29] There may be a metallic dome covering the whole of the planet, thereby denying tourists a decent view of a gran-diose perspective: 'There was no green to be seen; no green, no soil, no life other than man.'[30] With populations entirely concentrated in cities, the countryside becomes deserted, abandoned. Nature returns to its wild state; it is no longer cultivated; people live on hydroponically grown food and yeasts.

Structures Built of Greenish Borazon.

With the decline of the 'American' city in fiction, one finds, either in parallel or concurrently, other forms, other modes of organising life and human habitation. The vacuum created by a *tabula rasa* leads to the emergence of cities that are extraordinary and astounding. In this creative surge, forms and urban plans break free from historical and architectural reference points and from earth-bound terrestrial models. Henceforth people live in the air, underwater or in space. It takes a while before buildings break with the parallelepiped model and become circular, open to the sky. One can already see the future, and it consists of something other than machine-oriented living. There exist numerous ways of seeing and living the city.

These may involve the death of the city as we know it today, and a development of something quite different. In the geometry of the human environment and the way humanity perceives itself in relation to its living space, it may well have setbacks and heartbreaks in store, but there will also be surprises and unexpected pleasures. The materials are new: 'There rose a tubular tower made of steel, which supported two latticework arches. An enormous parabolic spiral in beryllium bronze, decorated with rhenium studs, was built at an angle, with its flaring edge opening to the sky. A second spiral, alongside the first but opening towards the earth, was built of eight large cones of greenish borazon.'[31]

The 'mechanicist' evolution of cities means that they are no longer built in natural, anarchic fashion by the juxtaposition of disparate structures and the absorption of old living spaces into the new; rather they are built *ex nihilo*, along rational lines, with basic building blocks being endlessly repeated if necessary. Electric generators produce anti-gravity fields that keep the city floating several kilometres above the earth. For all that cities may be suspended above

23. *Left: Behind the high speed highways of the new cities rises the tutelary silhouette of the American skyscraper. 1932*

24. *Right: A colossal city, entirely based on science, the mastery of the atom and the conquest of space. 1942*

the planet, or out in space, they still reproduce the classic Manhattan model of huge buildings with stepped top section, but now redesigned into a circular perspective.

The cities of the future are dangerous places; they promise ruthless competition, programmed leisure, aerial playgrounds and the hunting of human prey. In the poor quarters of Centropolis there were 'houses that had been built of plastic a hundred or more years before. Made of virtually unbreakable materials, their imperishable colours basically as fresh and bright as on the day of construction, they nevertheless showed the marks of time. Dust and soot had fastened leech-like upon the glistening stuff. Lawns were ill-tended, and piles of debris lay around.'[32]

Some of the dead cities portrayed are familiar to us. 'By the year 9000, Kentropol had become the principal city of the urban conglomeration which, following the terrible disasters of 8960, had developed along the coast of the Mediterranean, particularly on the African side.'[33] Some cities disappear in the wake of wars or climatic change. 'Paris rests in ruins. The silence of the grave weighs upon it. A dense and invasive vegetation

25. Aerial cities above the earth's crust 10,000 years from now. 1929

wraps itself like a tight shroud around this vast corpse of a city which no longer exists. Brambles and undergrowth hug and loosen any masonry that is still standing . . . The forests of former times have re-established themselves along a River Seine which flows broad and free, skimming past reedy banks and wearing away the mossy old stones sunk

in its bed. Peering through the oaks and birches, one sees marshes that have re-formed and lie glistening in the sun.'[34]

Other cities are deserted, but are still illuminated and apparently functioning. 'Lonely lights burned in the stores all day. The shop doors were wide, as if people had run off without using their keys. Magazines, brought from Earth on the silver rocket a month before, fluttered, untouched, burning brown, on wire racks fronting the silent drugstores. The town was dead. Its beds were empty and cold. The only sound was the power hum of electric lines and dynamos, still alive, all by themselves.'[35]

The first depiction of an aquatic city is as a floating island: 'Built of reinforced concrete, with an aerodynamic hull, it offers little resistance to wind and tides. The island has an engine which operates a propellor; this ensures that it stays in the same place, counteracting the effect of the tide. It has a large port at its centre, for the movement of ships and landing craft, as well as repair shops, lighthouses, and even a hotel for travellers.'[36] The spectacle of Atlantis is ever present. Perhaps it will be rediscovered on Mars, or some other planet.

Then there came under my gaze, about two miles below, one of the most beautiful sights I have ever seen: the soft, yet brilliant, radiance of the great Han city of Nu-Yok. Every foot of its structural members seemed to glow with a wonderful incandescence, tower piled upon tower. Philip Francis Nowlan, 1928 [37]

26. Below: The reader transported into the future. 1952

27. Right: Buffalo City, an American city in the 26th century. 1936

The new millennium has not always been viewed rosily. Some writers made it clear that there would be a price to be paid for progress, and chose to portray a posterity that had been

Fear

purged of naïve enthusiasm. There was a feeling that some of the bolder ideas for the future were suspect; hazy notions could be kept for later; the Golden Age would have to wait for a while. In a dirty future crowded with old demons, mothers unaware of the dangers end up giving birth to future executioners, and all kinds of bloody cohorts join the parade. The world could have turned out disastrously, but even negative Utopias have a chance of ageing horribly well. If we are to believe the baleful omens and prepare ourselves for the worst, then at least, when it comes, let us not be caught unawares, consumed by anxiety and succumbing to death, because we shall all have been warned.

The broad progressive movement that developed out of the Industrial Revolution tended to favour a univocal and optimistic view of the future. But, with time, doubts and questions began to be raised, and alternative points of view emerged, expressing nervousness about a future that some feared was going to be dreadful. In the twentieth century, a few voices were raised in the hopes of alerting people to the dangers of a future society which threatened to be a thinly veiled reproduction of forms of government which were to become, sadly, all too familiar; these voices also speculated on the likely development of some of the world's less desirable tendencies (the threat of overpopulation, the destruction of the planet's natural resources, mechanisation and the power of science). To bear witness to this bleak future, we have man projected into the future as he is illustrated on the cover of books and as he recounts his stories in nightmare tales where he is sent

off to explore, and where he does not know whether the facts which he reports back will prove to be portents of disaster.

Theatre of Horror. A variety of catastrophe scenarios portray the planet as a huge sprawling city, on the model of the conurbations of Japan and California. What still exists of the uninhabited world is desert, the very existence of which may not be apparent to the city dwellers, who travel from one place to another in aircraft which are huge, windowless cylinders.

The efficient functioning of these big cities depends on extraordinary systems of machinery and a highly precarious organisation of society. In this decor of gigantic, monstrous cities the human scale disappears, as does even the memory of the place that humans were once supposed to have occupied on earth. Jostled, crushed, forced into unbearable communal living conditions, the human being becomes lost.

In addition to the ecological death of earth there are other horrors in store. 'There was of course no way of knowing whether you were being watched at any given moment. How often, or on what system, the Thought Police plugged in on any individual wire was guesswork. It was even conceivable that they watched everybody all the time.'[1] Electric shock treatment for the mentally ill may be extended: 'In 2026, a wave of depression and pessimism threatened the nation and led to an enormous upsurge in divorces and suicides. On the advice of the Great

1. Preceding double page: The Machine, a fortress dominating everything. 1926

2. Far left: In the depths of foreign planets, monstrous and hostile cities will be built. 1935

3. Left: Criminals will be sentenced to aerial punishment. 1920

4. Right: The giant bunkers of Power. 1929

Medical Council, the Government took emergency measures. The whole population was required to submit itself for electric shock treatment. Men, women, children and old people alike went along for their regulation dose.'[2] In addition to fear, paranoia and loss of identity, there are physical aggressions. Sometimes the inhabitants of a city go so far as to accept mutilation in order to escape society's horrors. The suburbs become battlefields for mothers who now have the task of upholding clan honour.[3]

Evil. Evil powers join forces so that man and everything that justifies his life and his existence on earth is diminished and, in extreme cases, eliminated. Here the picture is uniformly bleak. Voltaire's philosophical tale *Candide*, in which he paints an ironic picture of 'the best of all possible worlds', is a clinical demonstration of anti-Utopia.

Fearsome cities are portrayed which are vertical, concrete and programmed. Society is imprisoned within them, and the workings of these cities serve the interests of those who seek to be masters of the world. A malevolent being — a dictator or perhaps a

mad scientist — represents evil, the anti-hero triumphing in a nightmare where no saviour arrives suddenly from the wings, and no avenger comes to bring justice. A descendant of the Malignant One of olden times, in science-fiction writing he crystallises the terrors of a Western civilisation that is all too aware of its shortcomings. On the one hand we have the clean-cut hero, who is public and extrovert; on the other we have the man of evil designs, cold, calculating and ruthless. Dictatorship plus controlled media plus cult of the personality: they play on a familiar theme. The stories often

portray a central computer with all-embracing powers over society; there is also the symbolism of the ever-present face of Big Brother, backed up by electronic surveillance, doctored news and other instruments of subjugation.

The man-machine, the absolute master, is not alone; his henchmen are there too — both human and mechanical — as obedient, blind instruments of a police or military order. It is undoubtedly easier, more logical and more literary to have evil intervening in the form of a particular individual, a person who can be made responsible for disasters. This Manichaean characterisation underpins the classical view, as does the struggle for hegemony between major power blocs, the cold war and the bipolarity of world politics. A more subtle depiction of the future has humans as actors in their own destiny, thus rendering them responsible for their own subservience. Some are governed by machines, by computers which they themselves have built and programmed as part of a coherent and generous vision of the world, a vision which in the longer term turns out to be negative, however, and triggers the total annihilation of humanity.

War is peace

Freedom is slavery

Ignorance is strength.

George Orwell, 1948[4]

5. *Left: War is pleasant. 1951*

6. *Above: The disintegrator gun in the year 2419. 1928*

7. *Right: An earthling in the hands of hostile extra-terrestrials. 1937*

There are other stories, other visions of the future, which highlight the negative elements present in today's society and those of any tomorrow which takes them as its model. Collectivism and totalitarianism equal blind government, the imposition of one-party rule, and the tyranny of public over private life. The role played by political ideologies in the production of human unhappiness is manifest: the totalitarian hells of Nazism, Stalinism and the iron heel of plutocracy. We find a depiction of a power that is capable of abolishing human values — values which are defended with a determination tinged with fatalism by a handful of individuals who have not yet been crushed by the 'steamroller', and who are unable to accept a happiness that is intolerable. The ruling forces may be represented as a social class, giving a different view of the time-honoured opposition between master and slave. On the one hand we have the rich, the 'Titans', superior beings, and sometimes a dominant sex, which may be female or neuter, and on the other we have the eternal poor, sub-beings, slaves, the cast-offs of the human species, resistance fighters, nonconformists and 'atavists'. In 2472 human beings are no longer to be found in Ireland; it becomes the island of New Amazonia.[5]

Like the ant or the bee, the human being exists only as part of a social grouping, and takes his place as a necessary but anonymous and interchangeable cog in the great machine. A sophisticated technique of dehumanisation uses a combination of mass media, propaganda and psychological warfare. Inquisition, coercion, the abolition of freedoms, and the military and police state are all there. And the nightmare is intercut with flashes of lightning and the sounds of blows.

Mad Scientists.
Another major threat for the years to come is science — a science in which humanity has, incidentally, placed great faith. It may turn out that man's future is dependent on the experiments

of scientists who are capable of the worst aberrations, along the lines of the master of *The Island of Dr Moreau.* In some cases the scientists' only desire is to enable their contemporaries to profit from recent discoveries: 'The progress of surgery was so remarkable that, on the slightest pretext, surgeons would remove the most delicate organs or relocate them. People had their insides cleaned every once in a while, which effectively left them with a brand-new body. The effect of the cure was, if need be, as much moral as physical.'[6]

Not all scientists were mad. In some cases, madness and revenge were synonyms for frustration. The scientists of the future may set aside metaphysics in order to pursue experiments relating to industry. Intelligent, logical and cold, utterly devoted to the advancement of their research, they come across as devoid of

8. *Perverting the course of science. 1926*

morality. With no concern for ethics, but also with no emotion or compassion, they become machines for calculating, researching, discovering, transforming and killing . . . All this is in the service either of their own ideas, or of a dominant being who is able to use them. The anonymous white coat which they wear to guarantee their absence of feelings. And they may easily be replaced or assisted by robots, given how easy it is to manipulate their pre-established programmes.

Creatures from Elsewhere. The malefactors of the future are not necessarily human. A multitude of exogenous dangers have featured in science fiction, centred on the archetype of the malevolent alien in all its variants. Western society, which is so unwilling to accept 'foreigners' either on its territory or at its frontiers, here exorcises its fear of the alien and projects it into space. But the extra-terrestrial arrives, green-skinned, disguised, close to animalism but nonetheless intelligent, in his inevitable flying saucer, or perhaps as part of an aerial flotilla swarming like a cloud of locusts. When they arrive disguised as humans, the strangeness of certain details

9. *The ineluctable, terrifying reign of the Machine. 1935*

In 2642, Doctor Warnod isolated the death bacillus and was able to conquer it thanks to his marvellous serum. Men became virtually immortal; earth was soon too small to house them all, and it was necessary to think of ways of disposing of the surplus inhabitants. The last law, which is still in force, is the law of District Sacrifice. The *Journal Officiel* carries details every week of which *arrondissement* is next in line, and the inhabitants are expected to report to the town hall before midday in order to be electrocuted.

Roland Dorgelès, 1919[7]

Félix parcourait la ville. Il cherchait un appartement, c'est-à-dire un endroit où l'on voulût bien l'accueillir.

Il grimpa le long d'un gratte-ciel qui n'en finissait pas. « J'aperçois de la lumière à une fenêtre du dernier étage. »

Félix, toujours semblable à lui-même, traversait une ville aux architectures étranges et survolée par des avions.

10. *Felix the cat and the stresses of life in the year 2000. 1935*

of their first 'encounter' becomes apparent only afterwards. For example, their highly controlled way of speaking: 'English seemed as familiar to them as their mother tongue; but all three of them spoke like perfectly trained singers, with a total control of their voice and breathing.'[8] Or their words 'came out sounding strange, as if they had no palates.'[9] Invaders, intergalactic beings, sinister strangers, well-meaning people who bring disaster in their wake, rogues of every sort . . . the portrait gallery is very rich. War may even be declared by an enemy who is actually vegetable, but inspired by murderous intent and endowed with intelligence.

A Litany of Disasters. The malignant forces that appear in the history of the future are the authors of catastrophes which rival in horror the historical calamities which humanity has experienced. Nothing new, perhaps, compared to reality, except that the logic is pushed to extremes. The eradication of the human race goes hand in hand with the transformation of earth into a desert, or even the total disappearance of the planet. Some stories develop the history of humanity in alternative directions; in 2419, the Mongols are masters of the planet and America lives its life hidden at the heart of a forest civilisation.

At one time, people used to think that the risks of war were in inverse proportion to the killing power of weapons: 'Is war still possible with modern inventions, these poison-gas shells which can be fired over distances of a thousand kilometres, these electric sparks, twenty leagues long, which can wipe out an entire army corps at one blow, these rockets which have been armed with microbes of plague, cholera and yellow fever, and which would destroy an entire nation in a matter of hours?'[10] However, there are numerous examples of planetary wars, which are grounded particularly in fears of a Third World War and of the absolute powers of destruction in the hands of certain nations. The balance of power is altered: world hegemony may now belong to Asiatics, or to Africans: 'The moment came when the two powerful and unified hemispheres of East and West took up arms, and there was civil war on the planet. All I remember is chaotic visions of fire, thunder and hell.'[11] In the event, the East won, and the world was ruled by a single government.

Among the various weapons of destruction, the most common is the notorious

11. *Captain Future, a fictional hero in the futuristic mould, captured by 'evil' green men. 1942*

'death ray', which may be electrical, atomic, anti-matter, or charged with a secret power. There is also the 'disintegrator' ray, which is 'a terribly destructive beam. Under its influence, material substance melted into "nothingness", i.e., into electronic vibrations. It destroyed all then known substances, from air to the most dense metals and stone.'[12] Equally fearsome is the 'harmonic gun', which gives off 'vibrations that created shattering harmonics in every substance in contact with the floor. Glass, steel, stone, plastic . . . all screeched and burst apart.'[13]

Among the various sequels to the Great Conflict, which is variously referred to as the 'explosion' or the 'great disaster', we often find a return to a primitive stage of civilisation, with an upsurge in religious feeling which is marked more by superstition than by mysticism, and a new age of obscurantism, evil and corruption.

Humanity, subjected to the effects of radioactivity, experiences a growing number of deformed births. 'These monsters (actually the product of gamma rays) were a major problem in post-war society. Freaks were liquidated and their mothers had their heads shaved. But freakishness was so widespread certain limits had to be accepted, e.g., up to three nipples and seven toes or fingers were allowed.'[14] In a stinking, devastated London, next to a plague-ridden stagnant, Thames, it is the rats that rule. Monuments that have survived are no longer accorded the same respect: 'Bastion West Side, famous last bulwark in the Siege of New York, was dedicated as a war memorial. Its ten torn acres were to be maintained in perpetuity as a stinging denunciation of the insanity that produced the final war. But the final war, as usual, proved to be the next-to-the-final, and Bastion West Side's shattered buildings and gutted alleys were patched into crazy slums by squatters.'[15]

They Are Among Us. The other side of this picture of destruction, nuclear war and the symbolic Third World War is the arrival of invaders from Outer Space, extra-terrestrials who are vengeful and technologically superior, capable of operating from a distance to destroy earth — the marvel of creation and the cradle of a perfect race. A word of advice to mankind from a friend: do not venture into space with your ludicrous gifts of glass beads. When it comes to cowboys and Indians with the extra-terrestrials, it is you who will be the Indian. Don't be surprised when they arrive on your doorstep.

Among the emblematic images of a civilisation under threat, we have earth destroyed from afar by Jupiter or Mars, and the Empire State Building being 'uprooted' and captured by an alien spacecraft. Humanity may be confined to earth by alien worlds which seek to devise means of protecting themselves. After having used 'sub-etheric hand disruptors' in the course of the war against the Earthmen, the Spacers set up an impenetrable barrier to protect themselves from illnesses.[16]

The Kanamites consider human beings as a species to be reared and fattened before they are finally eaten. At first, their aims appear remarkably altruistic. Their mission consists of 'bringing you the peace and plenty which we ourselves enjoy, and which we have in the past brought to other races throughout the galaxy. Once your world has no more hunger, no more war, no more pointless suffering, that will be our reward.' But their true motives are terrifying: their book *To Serve Man* is in fact a cookery book.[17] For others, humanity is seen as the equivalent of cattle; mankind may also be regarded as a race of vermin to be sprayed with noxious chemicals before earth can be colonised. The Vitons, for their part, fight humanity by horribly devious means. A number of human beings are kidnapped and then sent back

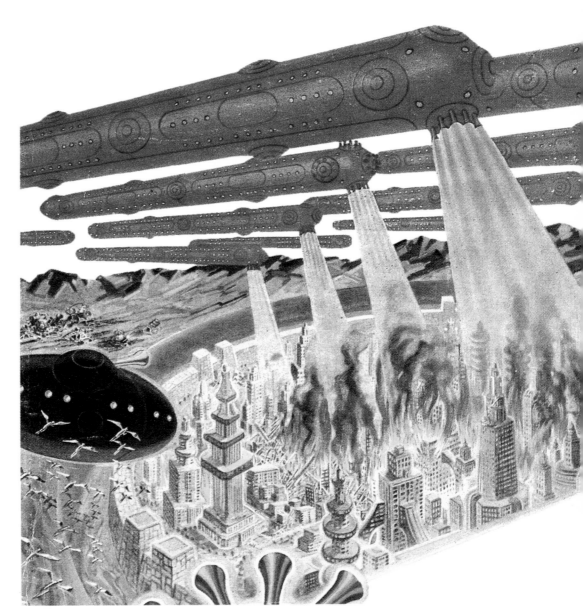

12. *The order was, simply, destroy. 1939*

He leaned forward to examine the scar on the young man's shaved head, a ribbon of pink tissue which ran in an unwavering line from the forehead past both ears to the nape of the neck. It was the welt that was always made when the dome of a troubled one's skull was sliced off with a Mandunga saw and then neatly pasted back in place. **Bernard Wolfe, 1954**[18]

among their people after a process of surgical brainwashing which instructs them to attack their fellow humans.[19]

The scariest of the extra-terrestrials is the one who cannot be distinguished from humans, because he has either assumed their appearance or taken over their bodies. Some capture the bodies of sleeping humans and take possession of them; others take the place of friends and family, having consumed their substance; there are also cases of extra-terrestrial children born to earth mothers. 'A white cylinder, a fleshy mass which sparkled like dew in the moonlight. An enormous cocoon made of a cotton-like substance. You could vaguely make out arms and legs, as well as an indistinct, half-formed head. There was not even a trace of a face. And yet Charles was able to say what it was. The embryo of a mother thing.'[20]

A Taylorisation of Time. What is predicted in these stories is not always the complete physical destruction of the human race; it may be civilisation which is in danger, at the hands, perhaps, of some despotic tyrant. Abolishing memory and handed-down culture is the way to abolish

14. *The horrors of warfare in the future. 1906*

13. *The spectre of the great atomic plague. 1912*

In the end they put to death all the criminals, the lunatics, the perverts, freeing the world of the dross which it didn't need.

G. Peyton Wertenbaker, 1926 [23]

history and links with the past. 'He recalled how our fathers had got tired of keeping these useless mountains of paper called "libraries", at a time when there was no place for cinemas either. Wishing to rid themselves of even the memory of the ravages of that appalling sickness called "literature", they had decided to burn all their books, down to the very last one. The age of chatterboxes was over.' [21] Some might see the banning and burning of books as a return to barbarism, but no, on the contrary, it would create a society that was mechanised, ordered and properly governed. Firemen see their job as a job of disinfection; the old books which they hunt out burn like dark weeds. All that remains now is condensed books, digests and graphs. [22] Oldspeak is replaced by Newspeak, which consists of the fewest words possible, and is regularly purged of shades of meaning and useless antonyms. 'Quite apart from the suppression of definitely heretical words, reduction of vocabulary was regarded as an end in itself, and no word that could be dispensed with was allowed to survive. Newspeak was designed not to extend but to *diminish* the

15. *A frightening vision of the future. 1950*

range of thought, and this purpose was indirectly assisted by cutting the choice of words down to a minimum.'[24] The strictest orthodoxy is preached for those 'who have no need to think'. On earth, and then on Mars, moral hygiene inspectors ensure that the law is obeyed. This 'is formal. No books, no houses, it is forbidden to produce anything whatever that might suggest ghosts, vampires or any other creature born of the imagination.'[25]

The experiments in tele-induction being conducted at the Zworykin Institute of Electronobiology are unsettling, to say the least, 'by reason of the hold that they may exercise over people's minds. In the hands of illintentioned people, greedy for power or seeking to impose their own personal ideas, it may serve as a means of propaganda, a word that is detestable to all.'[26] Elsewhere, we find the exploitation of people's psychological weakness by conditioning. 'Each sample of Coffiest contains three milligrams of a simple alkaloid. Nothing harmful. But definitely habit-forming. After ten weeks the customer is hooked for life. It would cost him at least five thousand dollars for a cure, so it's simpler for him to go right

on drinking Coffiest — three cups with every meal and a pot beside his bed at night, just as it says on the jar.'[27]

All kinds of methods of achieving automatic happiness are explored. Pleasure may be attained by means of drugs, 'soma', ersatz passion and by the provision of a ready-made life of ease. Alongside the systems of audio-visual conditioning, we find lonely people living next to each other and yet unable to communicate with each other: 'A great thunderstorm of sound gushed from the walls. Music bombarded him at such an immense volume that his bones were almost shaken from their tendons; he felt his jaw vibrate, his eyes wobble in his head. He was a victim of concussion.'[28]

In a perfect world from which evil and contradiction are excluded, uniformisation ends by creating what are effectively moral clones: 'You would think that you were surrounded by mirrors: when I look through other people's walls, I see myself, with my room, my clothing, my movements, repeated a thousand times. This makes you feel good; you see that you're part of a huge and powerful entity. It's so beautiful: not one useless gesture, inflection or movement!'[29]

Guinea Pigs in Test Tubes. In certain societies, pseudo-robots are developed on the basis of human genetic material, for example, the 'ectogenetic' children who are reared outside of normal family situations. 'Now psychological techniques made it possible for any human being, if caught young enough, to be conditioned for any role (below a certain level of achievement) which the rulers considered desirable.'[30] The future life of embryos is written in the Hall of Social Predestination.

Every kind of monstrosity is described. They may be the result of experiments where humans are imprisoned, tortured and subjected to degrading treatment; or they may be defectives who are eliminated in order to obtain a perfect society, a clinically pure race, and pliable minds.

Where once he was a monomorph, man now becomes a biological composite: 'We are all called "polyplasts", which means "the form of many". My name is 17,177. It's completely ridiculous, but I can't do anything about it.'[31] Elsewhere, industrial embryology replaces the old methods of human reproduction. 'The jars, each containing an embryo fed with artificial blood, were lined up on conveyor belts like

16. *Left: A terrorist will unleash death on a cosmic scale. 1953*

17. *Right: After the War of the Worlds, human beings will live in fear of invasion by extraterrestrials. 1939*

A THRILLING PUBLICATION

Dauphine cars at the Renault plant. It took exactly two hundred and sixty-seven days for the jar to go from one end of the manufacturing hall to the other, where, at each stage, it receives the necessary doses of hormones, DNA and RNA.'[32] The Bokanovsky process is an instrument of social stability, in that it enables one to achieve clones that are perfectly adapted to a predetermined future: 'A bokanovskified egg will bud, will proliferate, will divide. From eight to ninety-six buds, and every bud will grow into a perfectly formed embryo, and every embryo into a full-sized adult. Making ninety-six human beings grow where only one grew before. Progress.'[33]

Operating in the area of eugenics, euthanasia, the search for immortality and the degeneration of the human race, biological experimentation leads to the mutants of the future and the advent of higher civilisations, perhaps, but also maybe the age in which dogs and ants will come to take the place of human beings.

Psychological Surgery. The human being is the microcosm within which all these upheavals affecting the planet, the race and society as a whole take place, the micro-cosm in which they are reflected and take on a moral meaning — because the individual is the psychological anchor of fiction. The use of science or technology solves political and ethical problems, and the individual is the privileged vector of these processes. The hero, whether defeated or still fighting, comes across as the spokesperson and symbol of human civilisation. He may carry a reference number, but particular characteristics bring him to life within the framework of the story; a stroke of the pen, some tiny detail, gives him an individuality that provides the reader with something to hang onto in the face of the smooth walls of mechanised anonymity. Cruelty and destruction evoke a greater reaction when the victim is more than just a number.

People may be hunted down by robot detectives; they may be tortured by starvation, beatings, electric shock, the destruction of logic, the disorientation of their minds, and the acceptance that two and two doesn't make four, 'sometimes they are five. Sometimes they are three. Sometimes they are all of them at once. You have to try harder. It is not easy to become sane.'[34] The Party knows everything about everyone; the

18. *Above: Soldiers armoured like tanks. 1862*

19. *Right: Will we come to our senses in time? 1947*

The central globe was filled with a germinative plasma by means of which the human species perpetuated itself. From this came the eternal flow of life, which supplied labour for factories the world over.

Wallace G. West, 1929 [35]

20. *Above: Communal brainwashing. 1947*

21. *Left: Impotent in the face of rebellious robots. 1939*

THRILLING
PUBLICATION

22. A people without souls, without hope, without light. 1899

tele-viewer watches out for 'thought crime' at every moment, and you may even betray yourself in your sleep. The ultimate torture is to be confronted with the thing that you most fear in the world and to betray everything in order to escape. Then 'there are three stages in your reintegration . . . There is learning, there is understanding and there is acceptance.'[36]

Rather like social insects whose life, work and state of dependence are governed by a dictatorship of chemistry, in the future oppressive and tyrannical state the individual no longer exists, no longer counts; the individual is expected to melt into the norm. Society tries determinedly to eliminate the personality of its members. Men will thus 'be treated as equal and uniform, and the law of mechanical slaves will be applied to them. No allowances will be made for the fact that they are human beings. There will be automatic arrests, automatic condemnations, automatic amusements, automatic executions. The individual will come to be as absurd as a piston or a machine part that demanded to lead a life of its own.'[37]

The wound inflicted on people's personal integrity may be very discreet and stealthy. An extra-terrestrial falls into a time warp and ends up in the Mideastern Radio factory, where he builds a device which is in common use in his own future world. Disguised as the latest model of radiogram, the 'Twonky' has the effect of changing men's characters and eliminating their individuality : 'It's not so much a radio, more a monitor. In this other civilisation perhaps everyone has one, or maybe only some people . . . those who need them. This keeps them in line.'[38] Nonconformists are destroyed. People who have been indoctrinated are the best proselytisers of the new order, and it's not always necessary for force to be used. 'There lies before you the subjugation of unknown creatures to the beneficent yoke of reason — creatures inhabiting other planets, perhaps still in the savage state of freedom. Should they fail to understand that we are bringing them a mathematically infallible happiness, it will be our duty to compel them to be happy.'[39]

When the psychological element is explored, one finds disconcerting developments. For example, the spectacle of horror may provide aesthetic enjoyment in time travellers who view great events of the past. A composer puts together a symphony of terrifying visions of pain, sickness and death deriving from great historical tragedies: 'The symphony began with the meteor that had

23. *Caught in the giant robots' trap. 1942*

24. They will be guards and sleuths. 1953

preceded the great epidemics of the sixteenth century, and ended with the apotheosis which Cenbe had grasped on the threshold of modern times.'[40] Future society makes excessive use of hypno-television, of tele-psychic advertisement and psychomotive infrasound in advertising.

In the year 2300, esper (expert in extra-sensory perception) psychoanalysts carry out telepathic probes of people's brains at the conscious, subconscious and unconscious levels. All this may save time for ordinary people, but the situation of criminals becomes extremely uncomfortable. They may be subjected to neuro-shock: 'It's like the neuron scrambler but psychogenic.'[41]

Some people agree to let themselves be used for scientific experimentation, but the risks may be very great. Seeking to achieve immortality 'brings sacrifices. One must renounce love and all the pleasures of the senses.

This operation eliminates not only the simple fact of reproduction, but it also deprives a being of all the things associated with sex, love, the sense of beauty, the taste for art and poetry. It leaves only a few emotions, the ones which are egotistical and indispensible for the instinct of self-preservation.'[42]

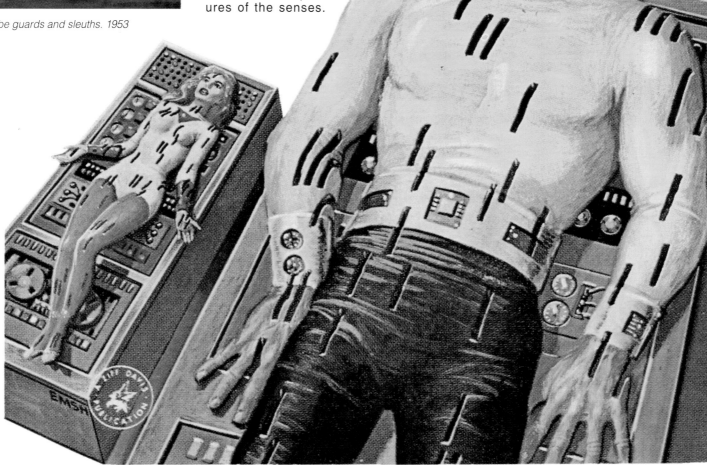

25. Being subjected to normalisation. 1963

Underground Deviants. Programmed, crushed and lost, man drowns and dissolves in the ultimate negative order, in the great computer. He obeys the Machine; he is sometimes even sacrificed to it. He is an intelligent slave and he concentrates in his poor hands all the hopes of the world. Resistance fighters become living books, hunted savages who associate in secret organisations. Refractory, nonconformist, how many will escape normalisation, con-formisation, lobotomy, 'the big operation'? This process may take the form not of an execution, but of a terrible annihilation followed by a rebirth: 'If a man's got the talent and guts to buck society, he's obviously above average. You want to hold on to him. You straighten him out and turn him into a plus value. Why throw him away? Do that enough and all you've got left are sheep.'[43]

The hero who is hostile to the negative world around him becomes a resistance fighter, a deviant. While he himself may be a conformist, he may meet outlaws. 'He knew that duty demanded that he reported

an atavist on the run. He was aware of the chaos that these individuals had caused in the past, in rousing people against the established order, in fanning the last flames of revolt in order to foment brief conflagrations, with their stories of beauty, love and freedom.'[44] Where we come across retrograde individuals who are hostile to progress, to automatic happiness, to 'soma', to ersatz emotion, to registration, we find that they are recruited from among the savages who live in reserves, or the 'consers' (conservationists), or mediaevalists and other such 'atavists'.

Sexual relationships are controlled. Fertility may be regulated, with the number of children and time of conception set by the

26. Beings from the future will throw humans into a time trap. 1938

authorities, based on the status, the physical characteristics and the genetic value of the couple concerned. It may also be eliminated, with the business of reproduction being carried out by machines, or by a giant nursery, and with Malthusianism as a necessary part of everyday life. 'We also predestine and condition. We decant our babies as socialized human beings, as Alphas or Epsilons.'[45]

Behind these rules lies a Taylorisation of the depositors of ovocytes, a clinical examination of gametes, and notions of eugenics. 'When applied to humanity, the eugenic method would tend to create races of men that were taller, better or worse looking, and also perhaps more intelligent. Statistically this is irrefutable; the descendance of a given number of higher individuals is going to be of a higher quality than that of an identical number of beings with lower mental capacities. In two or three centuries, by means of eugenics, one will finish by creating, if not a super-humanity, then at least an absolute humanity.'[46] On the other hand, it may be that specialised beings will be created whose only human characteristic is that of a particular human organ corresponding to a given function. Sexual characteristics may

28. *Human ants will be under threat from iron men from Venus. 1952*

end up being considered as useless: 'These days women work, act and think like men, and one sees many who actually look like men. We are perhaps arriving at the point where, one day, we shall be creating neuter people. Much in the manner that bees have worker bees.'[47]

After the nuclear Fourth World War, sexuality was controlled by religion and libido was modified, except among those who were known as the 'Hots', who were ruthlessly punished if they were discovered. 'After Purification men and women were allowed to copulate in the arena. Various influences, radioactive and guilt-psychotic, had reduced desire in a normal person to five weeks in the year, but only two weeks of actual mating were allowed.'[48] Given that sexuality retains links with animality, and is thus a leftover of primitivism, it may function as a catalyst of rebellion or growing consciousness; it may also be seen as a truly political act.

A deep fear is also engendered at the point of society's confrontation with robots, cyborgs and androids. They may be programmed to do damage and kill. They are instruments of horror, with no understanding of good and evil; they may also provide an illustration of future life without men.

27. *The mechanical verdict of the ruling robots from Tranerica. 1939*

29. *In any case, surveillance will never stop. 1911*

Stellar

Before it came to the point of being planned and programmed, the conquest of space may have had no sense of its own limitations, but already it had its heroes. Exploration was not a question of the time or the means, but of courage, and one fine day the stars would belong to those who were bold enough to reach out to them. The expectation was that by the dawn of the twenty-first century the solar system would already be conquered and mapped and the galaxy as a whole would be preparing to welcome its discoverers. Humanity would do the heavens a strange kind of favour by shipping its bustling business out into space and stirring the universe from its infinite silence. There was no doubt about it: it was either that or die. Albeit unacceptable, the second alternative would have been considered, but only in order better to convince themselves that they were going to have to leave. With the passing of the centuries, as human beings travelled further and further, they might have ended up no longer knowing in which part of the infinite could be found the planet of their origins.

epilogue

The appeal is irresistible. The challenge of the 'new frontier' continues to incite mankind to step beyond its capabilities, to leap into the unknown. And of all the 'unknowns', the future was one of the most sought-after. The project was one of driving back — at least at the conceptual level — the limits of the unknowable; to embark on the conquest of mathematical, physical, philosophical, psychological, metaphysical and temporal infinities. To fire flares into the mists of the unknown. Yet on the threshold of the year 2000, at the watershed of this anti-history of the future, this terrain is as intractable and ephemeral as ever. Its explorers have been many, following in the wake of Wells's time traveller, and their scenarios, whether expansionist, retrograde, dynamic, static, pessimistic or optimistic, may cut across each other, interfere with each other, cancel each other out or contradict each other, but, for all that, they safeguard the virginity of what the future holds.

Colonisers of Space. The conquest of the stars was at first a natural stage in the onward march of technological progress, and a subject for fascinated curiosity; then it

became a necessity, as mother earth came to reveal herself as too small for her inhabitants. The first step in the human colonisation of space was the voyage to the moon. The calculation of speeds, orbits and propulsive power, and the use of giant shells, or rockets, or Cavorite, or 'etheric' force, as the means to enable the traveller to escape from earth's gravity,[1] all this belongs to the archaeology of the pre-space era. The Selenit, we are told, was to be taken out into the Atlantic, whereupon, 'copiously ballasted with large quantities of lead, the apparatus — specially constructed to resist enormous pressures, both internal and external — will be sunk to a tremendous depth. Then, having shed its ballast, it will assume a vertical position and will rise to the surface, gathering speed all the time. The jet engines will be fired, and when the Selenit reaches the surface of the sea, it will emerge at a speed of about 50 metres per second.'[2] The technical detail is meticulous, whether it's the Selenit, the Stellarium, the Intégral or the X-207. An artificial moon will also be put into orbit. Its external skin will be made of brick, fused airtight by atmospheric friction; it will house a team of thirty-seven humans, both men and women.

1. *Preceding double page: To leave earth, to go as far as possible. 1936*

2. *Left: The first Soviet steps on the moon. 1957*

3. *Centre: Establishing Luna-1 base camp. 1964*

4. *Above: A spacesuit. 1929*

5. *The earth, homeland of interplanetary navigators. 1933*

Next comes Mars, our cousin planet, whose valleys people have imagined to be mysterious canals linking electric cities, Venus, the whole solar system.

'Everything is ready. The bulkheads of the Stellarium are made of perfectly transparent sublimated argine and have a resistance and an elasticity which formerly would have appeared impossible to achieve, and which render it practically indestructible. The craft's pseudo-gravitational field guarantees a stable equilibrium for humans and objects alike. We have quarters in which the total space available runs to about three hundred cubic metres; our load of hydralium will need to be sufficient to provide us with oxygen for three hundred days; our hermetic argine bulkheads will enable us to move around on Mars at earth pressure, with our air being supplied by direct or pneumatic transformers.'[3]

Expeditions like these will need specialised spacecraft, and teams capable of working in space. No problem: 'Specially skilled workers will build this floating island. They will do this by assembling parts brought up on lorry-rockets. To be able to work like this in interplanetary space, they will need to wear silver-plated beryllium spacesuits, and will move about with the help of small rocket-pistols.'[4] But the first astronauts may find themselves facing the risk of shipwreck. Or of death. A Martian kills the earth people who land on the red planet, after his wife had dreamed of their arrival: 'You're unkind. I didn't think him up on purpose; he just came in my mind while I drowsed. It wasn't like a dream. It was so unexpected and different. He looked at me and he said, "I've come from the third planet in my ship. My name is Nathaniel York. . . ."'[5]

There will be heroes and victims who are launched into space against their will: these may be criminals — prisoners, who will have been allowed to choose between two kinds of death: a death on earth — assured and immediate — or death in space — conjectural and unforeseeable. Convicts and the general dregs of humanity are likely to end up with the punishment of being sent into space, which will serve as an extra-terrestrial prison. We shall meet top-notch space pilots who have been horribly and irreversibly crippled by the effects of excessive acceleration.

Five years to the triple system of Alpha Centauri, ten to that strangely matched doublet Sirius A and B, eleven to the tantalizing enigma of 61 Cygni, the first star suspected of possessing a planet. These journeys are long, but they are not impossible. Man has always accepted whatever price was necessary for his explorations and discoveries, and the price of Space is Time. Arthur C. Clarke, 1962[6]

The prototype Venus rocket was piloted by a midget: 'The project stopped right there until somebody thought of that most perfect servo-mechanism: a sixty-pound midget. A third of a man in weight, Jack O'Shea ate a third of the food, breathed a third of the oxygen. With minimum-weight, low-efficiency water- and air-purifiers, Jack came in just under the limit and thereby won himself undying fame.'[7] If people decide to follow him to Venus, this will probably be the result of a promotional campaign giving highly coloured, attractive images of pioneer life. The reality of pioneer life, however, is that of brave people sentenced to a kind of group confinement for twenty or thirty years at a time, feeding on hydroponic food, and living in hermetically-sealed cabins.[8] The difficulties of the voyage mean that people are obliged to take drugs — Spaceoline, for example. 'Everyone needs it on the first space-trip; almost everybody needs it for the first dozen trips; lots need it every trip. Without it, there is vertigo associated with free fall, screaming terrors, semi-permanent psychoses.'[9] Sleep may be induced, if necessary, by inhibition of the central nervous system. In the cockpit of the space vessel, the regeneration of air is at first carried out by chlorellae, or microscopic algae; this is a stop-gap method while awaiting the invention of machines for purifying and recycling, or even generating, air. The psychological tensions of long voyages in confined spaces necessitate a strict control over both crew and passengers, in order to pre-empt disasters.

Time Out of Joint. Intergalactic voyages and the exploration of deep space immediately pose the problem of the length of voyages. 'It took the classic kind of rocket five years to make a return trip to Jupiter, double that if the target was Saturn, and twice as much again if it was Uranus — not

to mention Neptune. No conventional rocket had ever attempted to reach Pluto. A return trip to that planet would have taken more than ninety years. But the pilots of "torches" had reached that distant planet, and had set up the Persephone station.'[10] The theory of relativity has shown that in a given closed system (a starship, for instance), the tempo at which time passes diminishes as its speed of travel increases. This is 'Langevin's paradox': at 87% of the speed of light, time passes twice as slowly. At 99.5%, time passes ten times as slowly. This may result in a phase difference of just a few years, or maybe a chasm of a millennium. The time distortion involved in very long voyages through space turns voyages of exploration into irremediable exile, and transforms the members of the expedition into outcasts.

Thus part of a journey may go at faster than the speed of light, by using hyperspace. 'Travel through ordinary space could proceed at no rate more rapid than that of ordinary light (a bit of scientific knowledge that belonged among the few items known since the forgotten dawn of human history), and that would have meant years of travel between even the nearest of inhabited

6. *Far left: First departure for the moon in 2100. 1936*

7. *Left: Arrival of the flying saucer from earth on the Forbidden Planet. 1955*

127

systems. Through hyper-space, that unimaginable region that was neither space nor time, matter nor energy, something nor nothing, one could traverse the length of the Galaxy in the intervals between two neighbouring instants of time.'[11]

When one has lived for a long time on another planet, one has marked difficulties in returning to earth. Life in space will create a second nature, and space travellers will be dogged by a sense of strangeness, of 'gravitational expatriation', of instinctive rejection in response to going out into sunlight and the open air: 'It's Earth. It doesn't feel right. I can't get used to it.'[12]

Contact. The notion of encounters with extra-terrestrials supplies a myth which, contrary to all plausibility, survives despite the state of present-day knowledge. Man is balefully alone in the midst of more than 15,000 planets, and will remain so for a long time to come. There is no shortage of conjectural extra-terrestrial models which vie with each other in baroque, imaginative detail. 'I think that our incurable anthropomorphism made us imagine there were human heads inside their masks. The skin,

like everything else, looked bluish, but that was on account of the light, and it was hard and shiny quite in the beetle-wing fashion, not soft or moist or hairy as a vertebrated animal's would be. Along the crest of the head was a low ridge of whitish spines running from back to front, and a much larger ridge curved on each side over the eyes.'[13]

However, humanity will continue for a long time exploring unknown planets, as a prior stage to establishing a colony or even 'friendly' relations. During these explorations, people will be watching for the chance to make contact with living beings, whether intelligent or not, and the degree of friendship or hostility which these show will have a major influence on the lives of the explorers. 'The Zoomorph reacted with total indifference to long waves, to light waves from the visible spectrum, and to the longer waves of ultraviolet light, but at the start of the Ramières frequencies it began to give signs of agitation, and when we reached the Bussault frequencies, it shot off backwards at high speed. . . .'[14] It is often hard to describe the 'mineral curiosities' discovered, which seem to have a 'suppressed animal quality' about them: 'The surface of structures was

8. *At the end of the journey, the meeting with the Morlocks, degenerate humans from the end of time. 1959*

covered in part by a mixture of semi-transparent bubbles and a kind of polychrome mildew, in which red was the predominant colour.'[15] Elsewhere, illustrators have succeeded in creating all kinds of slimy archetypes, with long tentacles, bulging eyes (bug-eyed monsters) and scaly, green skins. There are microscopic and invisible beings too, and also the inconceivably large — the planet Solaris, for example, which is entirely covered by an intelligent ocean, contact with which lies beyond the capacity of the human spirit. 'The existence of the thinking colossus is a constant source of torment to mankind. Even when man has explored cosmic space in all directions, even when he will have established relations with other civilisations, founded by creatures who resemble us, Solaris will remain an eternal challenge.'[16] Extra-terrestrials and mutants fall within a well established tradition of fairy-tale creatures, the equivalent of wizards, elves and gnomes. Cinema tends to overplay this aspect.

9. *Extra-terrestrial abduction. 1947*

A first intelligent contact in space may turn out to be the joining together again of two halves of what, thousands of years previously, had been a whole: 'Here were two beings who differed in a number of respects: the air which they breathed, the colour of their skin, their language, their dress and their culture. They were as different as day and night. Humanity's pliant fabric had been worked by the passing centuries, until the point that they could no longer recognise each other. But time, distance and mutations could not change the basic fact that they were still men, still human beings.'[17]

Human beings occasionally come across extra-terrestrial civilisations which are in a phase of decline, or which may have been annihilated. Colonisation often turns out to be disastrous, as in the case of the explorers who dreamt of plundering Martian archaeology, or those who intended to impose a touristic uniformity on Cundaloa. What can be done with these places? 'We'll give them new names, but the old names are there, somewhere in time, and the mountains were shaped and seen under those names. The names we'll give to the canals and mountains and cities will fall like so much

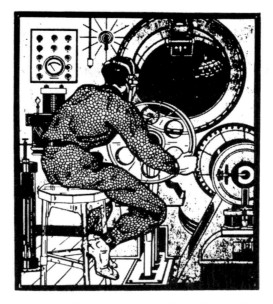

water on the back of a mallard. No matter how we touch Mars, we'll never touch it. And then we'll get mad at it, and you know what we'll do? We'll rip it up, rip the skin off, and change it to fit ourselves.'[18] The planet Skontar dared to reject the hand that mankind offered it, and by so doing saved its ethnic and cultural individuality from the alienation of the Solian system. 'You know the result. Dyrin's semantic came into its own, although the Solian scientists had written it off from the beginning. We built the tetrahedric vessel that all the human

engineers thought impossible to build, and today we cross the whole Galaxy in the time that it takes for one of the old space fleets to travel from the Sun to Alpha Centauri.'[19]

However, it may be that space nomadism will turn out to be barred to humanity, either for physical reasons of people's inability to adapt, or for political reasons such as their confinement by foreign forces. We find that at one point Mars invades earth, and that, at other points in its future history, earth is settled by beings who have been obliged to abandon their own planets. The Immortal, for example, a matriarch who ruled over Sarns and humans alike, came from the Forgotten World. 'The Mother of Sarn was not human. In the same way, her elf-like face was not human either. It looked strange compared to a human face, with its pointed chin and its tiny mouth, its golden eyes with slits for pupils, and the v-shape on her forehead, of hair that was not in fact hair.'[20] The External Worlds colonised by earth regain their independence, and become markedly hostile to any idea of an immigration of earth people, who are seen as bringing viruses and bacterias into their territory. Earth itself is in a bad state, suffocating under the pressure of overpopulation; it survives only because the big cities had been entirely mechanised. The solution involves sending numbers of earth people into space — the lumpen elements and the unemployed for example, who will be accompanied by robots — to conquer New Worlds.[21]

Life under the Domes. For the human who is not used to it, there are innumerable dangers on foreign planets: pressure, temperatures, liquids, the absence of atmosphere, etc. On Mercury, the traveller has to contend with the double hell of having one side of the planet burning hot because it faces the sun, and the other cast into an eternally freezing night. As a result, human settlements are established on the transitional ring, in low-angled light, in the eternal spring existing on the dividing line between the two opposing faces. On Venus it would be suicidal for the space traveller to attempt to follow the indigenous fish-men into the depths of the Venusian seas: 'They are chemically unstable. They always contain varying quantities of acid and a lot of chlorine. A vile concoction, but the natives seem to like it. They seem untroubled by the acids and the pressure and the chemical transformations, and perhaps they even find the smell agreeable.'[22]

There was, briefly, the picture of an unutterably bleak planet, low-mountained, sandy, frozen, everything frozen — Mars! There were pictures of a gorgeous glass-encased city, of great machines digging under a blazing battery of lights. Somewhere it was snowing with a bitter, unearthly fury. A. E. van Vogt, 1940[23]

10. *Left: Through the visors of their breathing apparatus, the Americans saw strange entities coming towards them. 1925*

11. *Above: Ralph, pioneering astronavigator, at the controls of his spacecraft. 1911*

The problems of human settlement in these places should not be underestimated: the fact that people didn't like the domes gave rise to the principle of 'terraformation': 'making the planets into near-images of the Earth, so that Earth-normal people could live on them. Port Earth was prepared to start small. Port Earth wanted to move Mars out of its orbit to a point somewhat closer to the sun, and make the minor adjustments needed in the orbits of the other planets; to transport to Mars about enough water to empty the Indian Ocean.'[24] Another scenario is proposed by engineers at Fowler Schocken Associates, with a view to establishing human colonies in space: 'A CO_2 blanket around Venus at forty thousand feet, approximately surface temperatures some five degrees a year, steadying at eighty to eighty-five degrees.'[25] But all this, of course, would be extremely expensive, and may turn out not to work. Thus the preference is for controlled mutations.

Intergalactic University. Human beings may possibly be required to submit to a series of tests, to prove their worthiness, before being allowed access to higher levels

12. *Left: Passion, risk and catastrophe during the galactic conquests. 1952*

13. *Centre: The survivors of the nuclear annihilation of the earth take refuge in the depths of the seas on Venus. 1947*

14. *Far right: Lost in the immensity of space for a journey without end. 1935*

If some stellar being with a superhuman psyche haunts our skies, we are still as powerless to discern its activity and to analyse its motives as a mouse would be to read scientific dissertations. Aimé Michel, 1962[26]

of space technology. 'Not all of these messages — not many, perhaps — will bring us comfort. The proof, which is now only a matter of time, that this young species of ours is low in the scale of cosmic intelligence, will be a shattering blow to our pride.'[27]

One day, human beings meet the Engineers of the Cosmos, who offer them a wonderful city. The earthlings turn it down, knowing that they are not worthy of it; but one day, when hatred and barbarism will have disappeared, then maybe . . . Some authors suggest that anybody who is able to create the technology required for interstellar voyages will have passed beyond the stage of military aggression. However, when the federal government of earth launches a spacecraft and sends it out beyond the solar system, it has on board an international, multiracial crew which, unbeknown to them, includes an extra-terrestrial whose job is to 'ensure that good representatives of the applicant race are brought here for an examination once they have perfected interstellar propulsion.'[28] They fail the exam. Elsewhere, the Extra-Terrestrial Federation of Planets arrives on earth and declares that there exists only one nation capable of fulfilling the conditions laid down for membership of the federation: 'In a place called the Kalahari Desert, on the African continent, there are people of short stature whom you call Bushmen. They meet all the conditions.'[29] An unrepentant anthropocentrism leads humanity to believe that there will always be a possibility of contact, of mutual recognition, of understanding; in fact the points of convergence, the interlocutors, may be so far removed that there is actually no basis for such certainty.

Endgame Scenarios. On the horizon of the future, which may be light years away or just around the corner, we find the spectre of death. It may be the end of our world, this 'modest village in the immense State of the heavens' of which Camille Flammarion speaks, or the end of the planet earth, or the end of human civilisation, but it may also be the end of the solar system and of the universe as a whole.

Literary end-of-the-world scenarios tend to organise themselves around major incidents: these may be cosmic accidents, like the tail of a comet passing too close

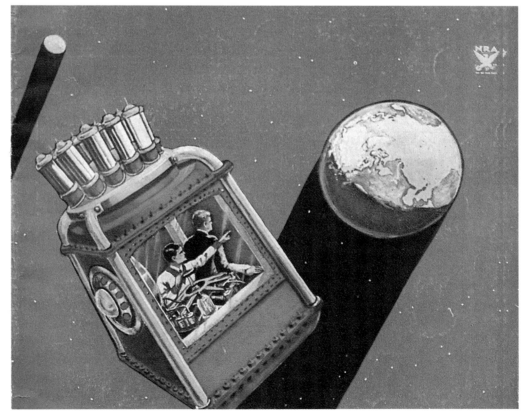

to earth, or climatic catastrophes, such as drought due to an exceptional heatwave, or major flooding, or the coming of new ice ages; the catastrophes may also be chemical, nuclear or biological.

Silence Reigns. 'New York, London, Paris, Peking, Berlin, Morocco, Japan, Andorra and the principality of San Marino were wiped off the face of the earth. On the model of Troy, Herculaneum and Pompeii, in 1985 the whole of the inhabited earth was buried under layers of ash, mud and ice. I say ice, because the temperature fell to 55 degrees below zero. An enormous hail of meteors and aeroliths and a rain of volcanic ash covered everything — towns and villages, hills and mountains, rivers and roads. Everything was hurled and battered about.'[30] The entire population of earth fled towards the equator, and subsequent archaeological excavations set about trying to recover the traces of ancient Western civilisations. Elsewhere, while flying over an ice-covered Paris, 'everything gave an impression of a tormented chaos, of a great fleecy flock of vaguely defined hillocks. A few things stood out. To the north and to the south stood two rounded hillocks, swelling with perfect and priceless precious minerals. Between them lay a valley, and at its bottom ran a smooth and winding ribbon, which must have been a frozen river, dotted with islands.'[31] And from the ice projected the shapes of Notre-Dame and the Eiffel Tower.

In its degeneration, in the headlong descent of its own mortal civilisation, earth 'will fall victim to exhaustion, or, rather, rendered eternally infertile by the folly of men, it will have a limited agricultural capacity, capable of feeding only degenerate races, which will vegetate in their old age, as in the primitive ages of humanity, in a state of barbarity and destitution akin to savagery. Thus the only people to experience the end of the world (or rather of the earth) will be a few scattered tribes, devoid of any degree of civilisation, and as animal as prehistoric man.'[32] As a result of overpopulation and the exhaustion of natural resources, man becomes a parasite of the earth that bears him.

It is quite possible that the disappearance of the human species and its much-vaunted civilisation will not have much effect on the planet. 'We have learned now that we cannot regard this planet as being fenced in and a secure abiding-place for Man; we can never anticipate the unseen good or evil that may come upon us suddenly out of space.'[33]

More than one catastrophe scenario has used the theme of humanity being destroyed by nuclear weapons. Mutants are cursed and reviled, being seen more or less as transmitters of deadly germs. 'The world had pursued its scientific progress until the day when, many centuries later, humanity itself was destroyed in a world war. Subsequently there were other cycles of living beings, in different forms, which in turn ruled the planet before themselves disappearing, like humanity, into dust and obscurity. There had been the cycle of ants, and the cycle of birds, as well as the Terseg invasion from Mars.'[34] Evolution may cease; however, after the great conflict, 'Earth survived. Almost all its living beings managed to survive; only men were missing. There were only a few tens of thousands left, and they assembled in order to attempt a new beginning. But the race's former fertility was a thing of the past; a mutation had taken place, and the results only gradually became apparent, as women succeeded in bringing fewer and fewer viable children into the world.'[35]

On the planet of the apes, the Simians are the superior beings: men are treated as laboratory animals, or as creatures for the

15. *Far left: A comet will bring about the end of the world. 1905*

16. *Left: L'Opéra de Paris under water. 1905*

17. *Below: When worlds collide a tidal wave hits New York. 1951*

The time it would take the head of the comet, which is 1,800,000 kilometres in diameter, to pass by would be 25,000 seconds, which is 417 minutes, or 6 hours 57 minutes. Fire would break out very quickly; our atmosphere would catch fire like a punch bowl. Camille Flammarion, 1905[36]

zoo. The human race has degenerated: 'What is happening to us could have been foreseen. An intellectual laziness overtook us all. No more books; even thrillers require too great an intellectual effort. No more games — mere pastimes, at best. Even the simplest of films no longer tempts us. During all this time, apes have been meditating, in silence. Their brains have been developing in solitary reflection . . . and now they're speaking. . . .'[37]

The Extinction of the Sun. 'Science had announced that the end of the world was due to arrive precisely on 3 April, in the last year of the Selenian era, at 5.27 in the evening. Humanity had been awaiting this date for a long time. Already, in the first centuries of the Rational Age, which came immediately after the Christian Age, the hypothesis of the final cataclysm had been the subject of scientific reports and investigations; but for 3,748 years now the date and the conditions of the event had been mathematically fixed.'[38] The end of the world is heralded by signs that are reminiscent of popular prophesies: 'There was an impression of darkness and a sense of

doom: colourless, soundless, beyond any anthropomorphism. When the poor peasants heard this oracle . . . from where had it come? What science, what observations of distant times, what memories of disaster did it represent?'[39]

The poisonous gas of a comet envelops the earth, bringing on mental disturbances, a great rapture and an extraordinary lucidity, followed by coma and then death. 'The great shadow was creeping up from the South like a rising tide of death. Egypt had gone through its delirium and was not comatose. Spain and Portugal, after a wild frenzy in which the Clericals and the Anarchists had fought most dreadfully, were now fallen silent.'[40] Elsewhere earth is destroyed by a collision with a comet: 'Our planet was caught in the tail of the comet, and as it turned in the midst of its incandescent gases, the movement of air stoked the fire, the sea began to boil, and filled the atmosphere with new vapours. A hot rain fell from the skies, the storm raged, electric lightning flashed, clouds of fire battled with clouds of water, rolling thunder tried to drown the howling storm, balls of lightning accompanied showers of meteors, and, with

the rotation of the earth, the general cataclysm gradually advanced until it arrived inevitably at the Antipodes, where the inhabitants, instead of being immediately consumed by celestial fire, died of suffocation by vapour, or by the predominance of nitrogen, or by poisoning from the carbon monoxide which had devoured all the available oxygen.'[41] The ineluctable march towards the end may be extremely slow: 'For five hundred centuries, men had occupied only derisory islands on this planet. The final degeneration had long been preceded by the shadow of decline. In ancient ages past, in the early centuries of the radioactive era, people had already become concerned at the loss of water: many scientists predict that Humanity will perish by drought.'[42]

Faced with the imminence of catastrophe, solutions are explored, but humanity (at least, most of humanity) has no access to an ark in space. The death of the medium-sized star which is our sun is not often the subject of projective writing because it is an irrefutable scientific fact. Hence there is no suspense. Authors tend to depict civilisation restarting elsewhere; however, new beginning may amount to an exile on other

18. Left: A space ark will save civilisation from a new Flood. 1939

19. Right: Watching the terrifying sight of the lunar satellite as it gets closer. 1933

20. *Death will come from the sky. 1950*

planets. There, having developed as far as the Eighteenth Species, humanity may have the privilege of having to watch the sun explode as a nova.[43]

The Day After the End of the World. Once the planet earth has been abandoned, either voluntarily or in the wake of a panic, there is often an 'after', and time may stretch or shrink, according to the author concerned. Here we are no longer presented with a history that is linear and Heraclitan, but with a multitude of possibilities, of cycles, of returns to savagery, of legends, of extraordinary technological complexities. In stories such as these, anthropocentrism loses a lot of its meaning, even though human beings still exist as a yardstick, and they may end up being modified, deified, or wiped out.

The human race has disappeared, but robot surgeons conduct experiments in 'homo-vivification' in laboratories, in order to create a human couple: 'He had to welcome them and help them to feel at home in this world which must have seemed so strange to their senses, which thus far had only been formed by prehistoric recorded tapes. At first

21. *Another end of the world. 1935*

it would be hard for them to adapt to a world peopled only by robots, with no other human beings.'[44] They are effectively orphans; they have lost contact, because of the huge spans of time and distance involved. Their mother planet is probably dead.

By a counter-balancing mechanism, we sometimes find that when earth is in ruins, or humanity has been decimated and civilisation is collapsing all around, a new colony is found, and Eden, or Terra, or New Sol is recreated elsewhere. As the exiles say farewell to earth and board the rocket for a hasty escape, they feel, despite themselves, that they are the repositories of a fragile treasure. But 'Dale had never shown itself to be generous, any more than the other colonised planets. It had killed the seeds brought by man before he was able to find ways of adapting them. And the native plants either poisoned those who tried to eat them, or repelled them by their vile smell. In the end it was necessary to turn to synthetic foods.'[45]

Debased versions of earth religions and mythologies transmit themselves down the ages. A far-distant memory of humanity still exists in the stories that are passed down

The intensity of the blue sun activated the inert minerals. Peaks, jagged ridges, walls indented with rocks, red like raw wounds or black like abysses, jutted out like the entrails of the planet. Lava plateaux swept by fierce whirlwinds were pitted with crevasses and trenches out of which seeped red hot magma, so that they looked like veins of bleeding fire. Ivan Yefremov, 1959[46]

from canine generation to generation: 'Of all the disturbing factors in the tales (and they are many) the most disturbing is the suggestion of reverence which is accorded Man. It is hard for the average reader to accept this reverence as mere story-telling. It goes far beyond the perfunctory worship of a tribal god; one almost instinctively feels that it must be deep-rooted in some now forgotten belief or rite involving the pre-history of our race.'[47]

The Last Man. The 'last man' may be the last representative of humanity *(homo sapiens sapiens)* and may be aware of his uniqueness. He will die alone and devoid of hope: 'It's strange to be alone, and to be so cold. To be the last man on Earth . . . The snow is falling silently around me, endlessly and depressingly. And isolated in this tiny hidden white corner of a misty world, I am without doubt the loneliest creature in the universe. How many millennia have passed since I last had real company? I have been alone for a long time. Before there were at least some beings of flesh and blood. Now they have gone.'[48] The individual may go as a free man to his inevitable death; at the point of death, he melts into the evolution of life in the universe. Night brings those stellar fires 'which had been seen by the eyes of trillions of men. There were now only two eyes left to contemplate them . . . Targ counted those which he had preferred to the others, then once again he saw the [moon] rise . . . and raised his sad hands towards it . . . He gave a last sob; death entered into his heart, and, refusing euthanasia, he came out of the ruins and went

22. *Left: A real hero will always save the interstellar pin-ups. 1965*

23. *Above: Mister Spock, of the starship Enterprise. 1965*

24. *Right: The earth, a desert. 1964*

to stretch out in the oasis among the ferromagnets. Then, in all humility, a few fragments of the last human life entered into the New Life.'[49]

The spiral of life, and the notion of humanity passing something on to another species, may be still more marked: for example, in the appearance of mutants and supermen. But man hangs onto his species like a drowning man hanging onto a lifebuoy.

The 'last man' may also be represented by a man and a woman — the last couple — setting off to bring fertile life to a devastated planet, or to unknown worlds, bearing all the hopes of humanity. It also carries the image of eternal renewal; there is the image of the brilliant fruit that may be gathered on Venus: 'Now, he remembered, he knew: the fruit of the tree of knowledge. From the world he had fled he brought the

only secret which it was important to know; he knew which poison, the source of all corruption, was contained in the red fruit. He jumped to his feet, reaching forward with his hand to push away the nightmare spectre of the future. . .'[50]

The theme of the last human relates to the end of terrestrial civilisations, and to the difficulty which Western civilisation has in conceiving of its own mortality. The process of degeneration is almost

always balanced in fiction by a move towards new things. In Asimov's *Foundation,* the scale of prediction is greatly magnified: 'Psychohistory, which can predict the fall, can make statements concerning the succeeding dark ages. The Empire, gentlemen, as has just been said, has stood twelve thousand years. The dark ages to come will endure not twelve, but *thirty* thousand years.
A Second Empire will rise, but between it and our civilization will be one thousand generations of suffering humanity.'[51]
One can follow the long chronology which traces the end of humanity as we know it, as created by Judaeo-Christian civilisation. Millennia

25. *Flash Gordon, archetypal conquering hero of the future. 1936*

after, this humanity gives way to another: 'Nobody any longer talked of Men-with-bronze-faces, or Men-from-the-country-of-the-snow, or Men-of-the-fixed-star; Earth now had only one people, the Andart-Iten-Schu, the Men-of-the-four-seas, who combined all other peoples in their own.'[52] This perception of human evolution, where we are perhaps only the 'iguanodons of future humanity', relates to Nietszche's phrase: 'Man is a rope stretched between the animal and the superhuman — a rope across the abyss.'

Fuel for the Stars. The extreme duration of intergalactic voyages means veritable generational spacecraft, in which the travellers who will finally arrive at the target star will be the descendants of the astronavigators who first set off. 'Even voyages which may last for centuries or millennia will one day be attempted. Suspended animation, an undoubted possibility, may be the key to interstellar travel. Self-contained cosmic Arks, tiny travelling worlds in their own right, may be another solution, for they would make possible journeys of unlimited duration, lasting generation after generation.'[53]

The voyage becomes a universe in itself. Various writers describe the travails of such odysseys — encounters with phantom spacecraft, astronauts getting lost or shipwrecked — and the creation of a whole string of legends. The individual loses his sense of a history measured against the scale of his own life, and becomes a cog in a giant temporal continuum. Other chronologies emerge, at incredible distances; era follows era within the intergalactic empire. Clarke believes that it will become impossible to write history, because of the breadth of the field covered by interstellar communications. Archivists and historians will be defeated by the time-scale, distance and immensity of the matter in hand. He says it will be impossible to produce a 'Galactic Encyclopedia', or a Yearbook for the Cosmos, since the number of volumes required would be enormous. 'Space can be mapped and cropped and occupied without definable limits; but it can never be conquered. When our race has reached its ultimate achievement, and the stars themselves are scattered no more widely than the seed of Adam, even then we shall still be like ants crawling on the face of the earth. The ants have covered the world, but have they conquered it?'[54]

26. *Buck Rogers's rocket in the 25th century. 1934*

This delicate glass roof replaces the thick atmosphere of earth. It has several very important functions. It allows into the city only the proportion of solar radiation which also reaches the surface of the Earth; it stops the portion which is stopped by Earth's atmosphere, and contributes to its transformation into electric energy; it protects against falling of meteorites, etc.
Sergey Gouchtchev, 1959[55]

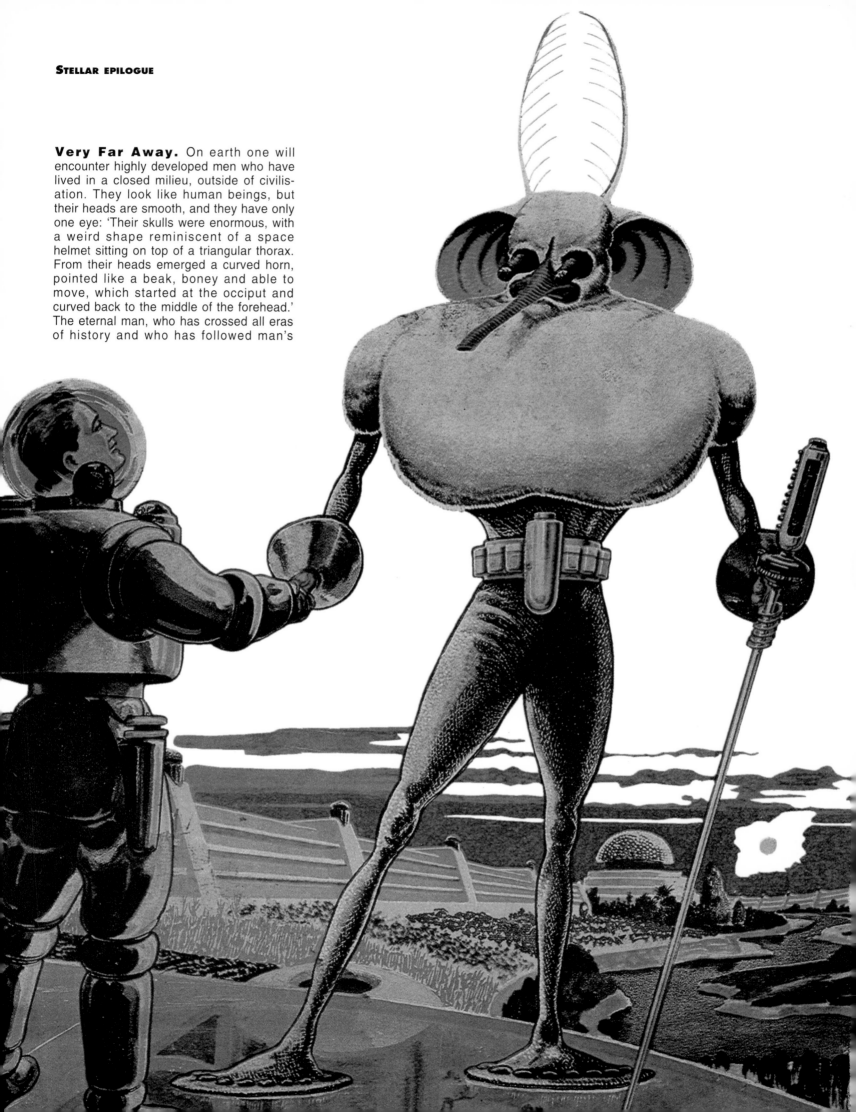

Very Far Away. On earth one will encounter highly developed men who have lived in a closed milieu, outside of civilisation. They look like human beings, but their heads are smooth, and they have only one eye: 'Their skulls were enormous, with a weird shape reminiscent of a space helmet sitting on top of a triangular thorax. From their heads emerged a curved horn, pointed like a beak, boney and able to move, which started at the occiput and curved back to the middle of the forehead.' The eternal man, who has crossed all eras of history and who has followed man's

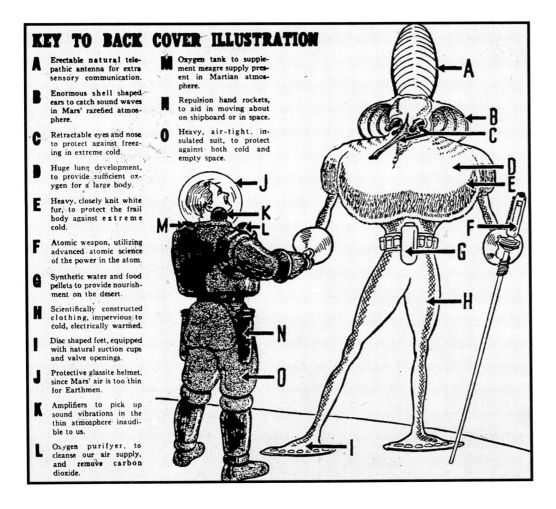

KEY TO BACK COVER ILLUSTRATION

A Erectable natural telepathic antenna for extra sensory communication.

B Enormous shell shaped ears to catch sound waves in Mars' rarefied atmosphere.

C Retractable eyes and nose to protect against freezing in extreme cold.

D Huge lung development, to provide sufficient oxygen for a large body.

E Heavy, closely knit white fur, to protect the frail body against extreme cold.

F Atomic weapon, utilizing advanced atomic science of the power in the atom.

G Synthetic water and food pellets to provide nourishment on the desert.

H Scientifically constructed clothing, impervious to cold, electrically warmed.

I Disc shaped feet, equipped with natural suction cups and valve openings.

J Protective glassite helmet, since Mars' air is too thin for Earthmen.

K Amplifiers to pick up sound vibrations in the thin atmosphere inaudible to us.

L Oxygen purifyer, to cleanse our air supply, and remove carbon dioxide.

M Oxygen tank to supplement meagre supply present in Martian atmosphere.

N Repulsion hand rockets, to aid in moving about on shipboard or in space.

O Heavy, air-tight, insulated suit, to protect against both cold and empty space.

evolution, remembers seeing 'curious beings, these men of the Cth century, with enormous brains on small shrunken bodies, with atrophied limbs, with slow, clumsy movements as they use small devices to help themselves move around.'[56]

Once the age of the first contacts is past, inter-world relationships become more complex. On the planet Siren, an extremely sophisticated code of relationships is in operation, and the Sirenians, who are always masked, communicate only by means of musical instruments, the use of which is very strictly regulated. The language translates the spiritual and emotional state of the speaker: 'Furthermore, they converse in a singing mode, and the person speaking accompanies himself on a small musical instrument. It is thus very difficult to evaluate the objectivity of factual information provided by a native of Fan or of the forbidden city of Zundar. They use a variety of instruments, and the stranger will be regaled with elegant arias and astonishing demonstrations of musical virtuosity. Therefore, when a visitor travels to this fascinating world, if he doesn't want

27. Far left: Encounter of the Third Kind. 1939

28. Left: A few details about a strange character, 1939

Extra-terrestrials and humans were capable of forming friendships. They could also be mortal enemies. Each species was, involuntarily, a terrifying danger to the other. And the only way of eliminating a danger is to destroy it. Murray Leinster, 1945[57]

to be treated with complete contempt he will have to learn to express himself in accordance with local customs and usages.'[58] Questions of language, of contact, and of aggressivity enter a new realm of meaning; these highly developed beings 'switch on' telepathically to the brain of their interlocutors in order to assimilate data regarding their culture and, *a fortiori*, their language.

Interplanetary voyages become more frequent and better controlled. On some planets the possibility of organising pseudo-terrestrial life appears too slim, so it is the humans themselves who have to be adapted to be able to live there. 'Sweeney was an Adapted Man — adapted, in this instance, to the bitter cold, the light gravity, and the thin stink of atmosphere which prevailed on Ganymede. The blood that ran in his veins, and the sol substrate of his every cell, was nine-tenths liquid ammonia; his bones were Ice IV; his respiration was a complex hydrogen-tomethane cycle.'[59] Pantropic treatment began

with conception, and was irreversible. A major programme of seeding of the universe was undertaken; recently discovered planets were peopled by humans adapted to live there. Mutations were happily accepted. People who were seduced by the wonders of life on Jupiter disappeared as humans, because their human essence dissolved into their new identity.[60] Mechanised human society may evolve in the direction of insects; the male sex is reduced to the status of a fertility machine, and then to that of an archaeological monster found only in museums. 'M-1 cursed the fate that meant

that he wasn't born a woman. He gazed with envy at the crowd of women workers with flat chests and slender thighs who crowded around the cage to gaze curiously at him.'[61] The first mutants, who were telepathic, were persecuted, like the Slans. But other mutants appeared, who owed their existence not to nuclear war but to bombardment by cosmic

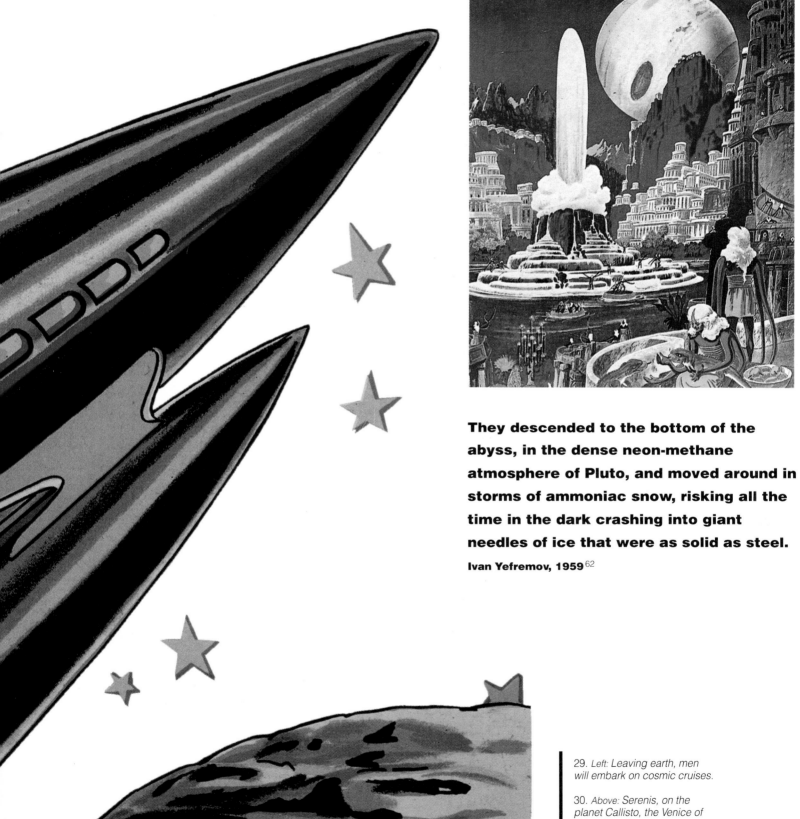

They descended to the bottom of the abyss, in the dense neon-methane atmosphere of Pluto, and moved around in storms of ammoniac snow, risking all the time in the dark crashing into giant needles of ice that were as solid as steel.

Ivan Yefremov, 1959 [62]

29. *Left: Leaving earth, men will embark on cosmic cruises.*

30. *Above: Serenis, on the planet Callisto, the Venice of Other Worlds. 1941*

particles in space, or to other non-identified factors. It was important 'never to lose sight of the fact that the majority of human beings were no longer "normal", and that there were increasing numbers of anomalous varieties. One found twelve main types: True Telepath, Levitator, Pyrotic, Chameleon, Nocturnal, Malleable, Hypno, Supersonic, Mini-Engineer, Radiosensitive, Insectivocal, Teleport.'[63]

In the age of the Great Ring, on their intergalactic viewing screens, 'everyone saw a man with grey skin and round, owl-like eyes which were ringed with a silvery down. He was of medium height, and very slender, with long limbs like tentacles. After a grotesque raising of his head, which looked like a hasty greeting, he fixed his impassive eyes on the screen and opened a lipless mouth, which was surmounted by a flap of soft skin in the shape of a nose. Soon the melodious voice of the translating machine began to communicate his words.'[64] The age of spirit having taken over from the age of matter and energy, intelligent creatures would be found everywhere in space.

31. *Eternal wanderers of the war of the stars.* 1931

WAKE ME IN A THOUSAND YEARS FROM NOW

If the current prospect of earth's final destiny is no longer a violent end, but a long-term decay, then the most confident of our peers must be those who have decided to take advantage of technological advances to have their bodies frozen. When they die, they will be kept in a state of quasi-hibernation in cryogenic containers stored in deep, earthquake- and bomb-proof vaults. Their bodies will be maintained at low temperatures, in blueish inert light, with white-coated technicians watching over them. Every possible step will be taken to ensure the preservation of these clinically dead envelopes of flesh. These old corpses have gambled what was left to them on humanity's ability to research and discover. As long as they are not forgotten, and as long as nothing untoward happens during the coming centuries to trouble their 'sleep', they will simply wait — and they won't even experience disappointment, having already stipulated that they should only be brought back to life as and when humanity has discovered how to do it. It would have been an entertaining idea to set their return date for around the year 2000, but this would have given too little time, and anyway there is no reason to be impatient. So, thus far the only way that we have of exploring the future is to get ourselves frozen. The process has not been perfected yet, and the reawakening promises to be difficult, but while there are no guarantees as regards the clinically dead, there is no reason to think that it will be impossible to revive people who have been frozen while still fit and healthy. So maybe this will be the only chance we have of finding a way to see the light of day under future suns. The year 2000 seems a bit too close now — but another thousand years would have a treat or two in store.

At the opposite extreme to these people whose 'existence' depends solely on machines, there are others who reveal a penchant, which one might find bizarre, for a complete return to nature. People's fascination upon discovering those rare human beings who have never left a state of nature relates back, as in the myth of our loss of the original Eden, to an immemorial past when we lived in a state of natural happiness. There is something saddening, as well as wonderful, in those animals that are defined as 'technophile' — certain species of rats and seagulls, for example. These species have adapted their behaviour to the modifications induced by mankind in their environment. These traitors to the fauna have discovered that this new rhythm, in short circuit with the human biomass, was ultimately preferable to the old ecological cycle. These ingrates of nature owe their survival to the fact of a strange alliance, and one might say that it is no mean feat.

There was a time when progress was obligatory, when men too had no choice about whether they liked this 'civilised' world, or whether they were

technophile or whether they had to be helped to become so — they had inevitably to submit. The neat thing about the year 2000 was that it made people forget that the 'Golden Age' was a thing of the past, and suggested that, with the assistance of machines, they would perhaps never need to work again, except to gather fruit and flowers. While people awaited this age of harmony, the most exciting thing would be the transition, the period of action which would prepare and reveal the coming of the Golden Age.

So much for living in the age of telecommunications, or the age of the splitting of the atom, or of artificial intelligence; rather, we find ourselves in a planetary iron age. We are the same people as fifty or a hundred years ago, with our same states and our same gleaming machines, some of which were imagined, and others which never were. The person who, one day, will describe the end of this last century will not have an easy task. The ongoing actuality which, for a time, for a lifetime, in fact, we pass through, has become our only mode of describing things. Where once we had an immediate, global perception of the world, now we have only simulation and spectacle, the intuition of the instant. The importance of any given event is a function of its dramatic intensity and how directly it reaches us. Simultaneity and emotional impact take the upper hand over analysis and grip both thought and movement within their empire. In the precision-measuring of time and distances, the perfect stationing of satellites, the interconnections of a million networks, each individual fact finds itself isolated in a flood of millions of others. We no longer retain anything of flows. With its label reading 'zero default', digitalisation replaces truth; in the real-time world, tragedies are numerical.

Time passes and overturns our myopic predictions by its incessant bifurcations and its unexpected trajectories. This is what is so wonderful about the future: one knows practically nothing about it. Anything that we presuppose is quite liable never to happen, or, worse, to turn out different. All kinds of horrors still arise from these thick mists into which we peer so nervously, continuing to feed a mystery, a parasite which has us gripped by our biological clock and never lets us go.

Now that the end of the millennium has allowed us to view it as it has actually turned out, with its exploits fixed in time, the small amount of future which is left to us, the trajectories which were taken and the tendencies which were accentuated, seem rather ridiculous in the light of the initial dream — what there was, and what no longer needs doing.

So, everything has happened very fast and very powerfully over the period since science began to accompany us through history. We have only just got over the discovery that we don't live at the centre of the universe, but that we occupy just one small part, no better than any other, on the outskirts of an entirely normal solar system in the suburbs of the Milky Way. We've had to face the facts: in this new milieu we are a bit out of our depth. The duration, the dimensions, the energy and perhaps also the complexity of the universe is all beyond us. We have been obliged to accept that the process of exploring space is going to be inhumanly slow. Now that the interstellar dream has become less immediately feasible, we are to remain prisoners of the green and blue gravity of a globe which is boundless but not infinite, wandering up and down without ever encountering a barrier, but at the same time with the virtual impossibility of ever being able to escape.

Planet earth, which has now been thoroughly mapped and explored, carries beneath its clouds a massive living wealth, for which reason it remains the sole vessel in space. However, from this extraordinary ark, despite its small size and its isolation, we are continually signalling our presence — and this by a means which is more rapid than the most adventurous of our little rockets. Radio and television transmitters use radio waves in order to communicate their programmes from a powerful worldwide network of transmitters, satellites and relays. It turns out that this transmission system leaks; every time a transmission takes place, some part of the signal is lost and ends up in space. This residual electromagnetic radiation which escapes in the course of radio transmission forms a cloud of particles which has been continuously expanding to the point where it now envelopes the earth. Once the electrons succeed in escaping from the atmosphere which held them prisoner, they begin to travel away from their terrestrial source, in all directions and extremely fast. Over time, they have travelled enormous distances and have created an electromagnetic radiosphere which is now assuming major proportions.

After so many years of intensive radio and television transmission, the range of this radiosphere must by now be approaching something like forty light years — four hundred thousand billion kilometres (40 x 101³). Thus, for all that our planet may be isolated and unknown in the greater scale of the universe, the fact is that it is unique. Planet earth has become a remarkable astronomical object: a planet with its own temperature of luminance. This value, which astrophysicians usually only attribute to the natural radioactivity of stars, this exceptional brilliance, is our celestial signature. The universe is being filled by the talking voices of a living species which, without necessarily intending it, has transformed its planet into a cosmic beacon: today planet earth has become a lighthouse, miniscule but findable, which 'shines' like a small sun, but in a fairly cold register, below the frequency of light.

Seen like this, the universe seems less busy than it actually is. First, on an extremely low frequency, we have the echo of the initial big bang; then the stellar throbbing of the black holes; then the ultra-fast tempo of pulsars, the crackle of neutron stars and of all those things which we can't see but whose natural and mysterious activity we can detect. Matter is working hard in all the various corners of space; we are bombarded by it. We often suppose that any creature from outer space who will have reached a level of scientific development similar to ours on earth will be able to pick out a distinct noise from amid the din of the universe : the artificial, random noise of human 'radio activity'. Its signal strength may be relatively weak, but it is nevertheless strong enough for the transmission to be identifiable, even after a voyage of many years. The signal which you receive on your radio can also be received by others, albeit distorted and with a time delay, far off in space. Already hundreds of solar systems are bathing in this radiation emanating from earth; our electronic dust has become a king of interstellar pollution. Puzzled extra-terrestrials will be receiving the signals of the TV parlour games, films and love songs that we are transmitting in their direction as if in an effort to give them advance notice of our habits and customs. By now they'll know us as we really are, and not just as we would like to appear.

But there is nothing immortal in the universe; the universe itself has a history, a beginning and an end. Once they exist, all newly organised systems, be they stars bursting into life or simple assemblies of interlinking molecules, obey the law of entropy, and operate under a countdown of one sort or another; all systems wear out, degenerate, and lapse ultimately into disorder, whereupon the elements that comprise the old system rearrange themselves into a new system. Everything that exists does so within time, and in the cloud of our radiosphere the electronic particles fade less slowly than our memory of the news that they transmit. Thus the wars and the revolutions that have been spoken about on radios and the deaths, the sufferings and the great passions which reach us by means of television — all this travels through space: at speeds of up to 200,000 or 300,000 kilometres per second, the time and distances involved take some computing. Space is so huge that when suns die or explode or coalesce into slowly darkening lumps, the news of their catastrophe reaches us only after an enormous delay. The light which reaches us from the stars is old; the sky that we see is an old sky. And our cloud of stories will travel for a long time, for astronomical durations of time in fact, and not encounter anyone likely to take an interest. And when it finally does, it will tell the stars in real time of events that happened eons previously. Further on, perhaps ten thousand light years from here, our sun appears the way it did when mankind had only just peopled the earth. Our radioactivity has not yet reached that far, and it won't do so for a long time yet. Then, when it's all over for us, those who gravitate around those newly unreachable stars will be sad, with the passing of the centuries, not to know how the story of our terrestrial humanity ended — assuming, of course, that they were interested in the first place.

Striking moments follow each other, one after the other, causing hopes to take flight and then shrivel away — signals indicate an imminent toppling over of history, hundreds of instants, all of which seem to be, and always will seem to be, harbingers, yet they turn into nothing, or perhaps only into bad news, and stand forever as eternal preliminaries to a new world. In terms of human progress, as in nature, 'everything that develops, grows and blossoms does so in the tiniest detail, gradually, and in tiny steps, whereas the big changes are catastrophic. But nobody is fired by a prospect involving tiny steps.' (Paul Watzlawick) When, by our complacent credulity, we clothed science in the attributes of mythology, we allowed it to shed its basic requirements of rigour and caution; all that was left of science was the adventure of discovery, the drunkenness of achieving understanding, a kind of predisposition to hope. The year 2000 became our 'vanishing point', when human progress would have been ready, at last, to accede to Humanity; this year stood out from the accumulation of centuries; its singularity conferred on it a real substance which gave it the power to negate inevitability. Nowadays it is only inevitability that rules. Heroism is no longer the tune of our times; people have no place for heroic visions of the future.

Projection into the future required a perfect instant. The year 2000 offered an ideal outer limit, an attempt to found a heaven on earth, to contain it at the furthest end of the century, and, with the passing of the years, having fought our way through difficult and glorious undertakings, to achieve the summits of peace and wisdom which we had promised ourselves. Like some great over-used toy, the year 2000 will turn out not to have been the lighthouse which should have led us through the century's night to the visionary limits of the wise men of old. To extrapolate is to dare to deduce . . . already the new millennium is starting a few years early, perfectly biospheric, in a universe of infinite space which ultimately has no measure but time and in which life offers a prospect of teeming interactions. Sedentary pixels, nomadic spirits; islands in space and time — that is what we have become.

NOTES

A general bibliography on the history of the future is beyond the scope of this book. Readers seeking additional sources are referred to the works cited in the notes to the Introduction, many of which include extensive bibliographies. References to these titles are not repeated in the list of Works Cited, which includes only the citations in chapters 0 to 5.

Introduction
1. A.-C. Decouflé, *L'An 2000, une antihistoire de la fin du monde*. Paris: Gallimard/Julliard,1975, 14-40.
2. P. Versins, *Encyclopédie des voyages extraordinaires, de l'utopie et de la science fiction*. Lausanne: L'Age d'homme, 1972.
3. P. Sipriot, *Ce fabuleux XIXe siècle*. Paris: Belfond, 1990, 5.
4. B. Cazes, *Histoire des futurs: les figures de l'avenir de Saint Augustin au XIXe siècle*. Paris: Seghers, 1986, 58-59.
5. H. G. Wells, *Anticipations, or the influence of mechanical and scientific progress on human life and thought*. London: Chapman & Hall, 1901, vol. LXIX, 747-760, 925-938, 1104-21.
6. B. Cazes, op. cit., 66.
7. G. Lapouge, *Utopie et civilisations*. New ed. Paris: Albin-Michel, 1991.
8. B. Cazes, op. cit., 81.
9. A.-C. Decouflé, *Les Millésimes du futur: contribution à une bibliographie des anticipations datées*. Paris: Laboratoire de prospective appliquée, 1978, 1.
10. A.-C. Decouflé, *L'An 2000 . . .*, 54.
11. E. Calvet, *Dans mille ans*, Paris, 1884.
12. Alfred Bester, *The Demolished City Man* (1952). Harmondsworth: Penguin, 1979.
13. C. D. Simak, *City*. London: Weidenfeld & Nicholson,1952.
14. J. Moselli, 'La Fin d'Illa', *Sciences et Voyages*, 1925.
15. G. Lista, 'La Représentation Futuriste de l' Architecture', exhibition cat. for 'Images et Imaginaires d'Architecture', C.C.I., Centre G. Pompidou, Paris, 1984, 43.
16. F. Choay, *L'Urbanisme, utopies et réalités*. Paris: Éd. du Seuil, 1965, 33.
17. Y. Christ, *Paris des utopies*. New ed. Paris: Balland, 1977, 27.
18. *Les Visionnaires de l'architecture*. Paris: R. Laffont, 1965; F. Choay, op. cit., 54-58.

Chapter 0
1. H. G. Wells, *The War of the Worlds*. London, 1898, 4,5.
2. C. Danrit, *L'Invasion noire: la guerre au vingtième siècle*. Paris, 1919, vol. 1, 15.
3. A. Robida, 'La Guerre au vingtième siècle', in H. Beraldi, *Un caricaturiste prophète*. Paris, 1916, 49.
4. 'Dans la nuit à travers les airs', *Lectures pour tous*, 15 Feb. 1914, 916-917.
5. P. d'Ivoi and Colonel Royet, *La Patrie en danger: histoire de la guerre future*. Paris, 1904, 1131.
6. 'Le Crapouillot en l'an 3000', *Le Crapouillot*, special issue, Christmas 1919, 3.
7. B. Wolfe, *Limbo 90*. Harmondsworth, 1952, 35.
8. Robida, *Le Vingtième siècle*, Paris, 1894, 357.
9. I. Yefremov, *Andromeda, A Space-Age Tale*. Moscow, 1960, 60.
10. J. Atkins, *Tomorrow Revealed*. London, 1955, 20.
11. *Science et vie junior*, no. 32, Dec. 1991.
12. *Cap and Bell: Punch's Chronicle of English History in the Making*. London, 1972, 203.
13. Henriot (H. Maigriot), *Paris en l'an 3000*. Paris, 1912, 19-20.
14. A. Robida, *Le Vingtième siècle*, 16.
15. P. Adornier, *La Mort du Film* (1926), *Ailleurs et demain a vingt ans*. Paris, 1990, 75-76.

16. A. Maurois, *Deux Fragments d'une histoire universelle, 1992: fragments d'une histoire générale publiée par l'Université de Tombuctou*. Paris, 1928.
17. H. G. Wells, *A Modern Utopia*, in *The Works of H. G. Wells*. London, 1925, vol. IX, 13.
18. A. Kyrou, "Vive l'an 2000: ses avions sans pilotes et ses briquets atomiques', *Actuel, 50 idées-100 livres qui ont frappé le monde*, special issue, Apr. 1989.
19. *Science et vie junior*, op. cit.
20. Robida, *Le Vingtième siècle*, 42.
21. *Science et vie junior*, op. cit.
22. J. Rostand, *Pensée d'un biologiste* (1954). Paris, 1978, 59.
23. P. Ferréol, *La Prise de Londres au XXe siècle*. Paris, 1891, 53.
24. H. G. Wells, *The First Men in the Moon*. London, 1901, 288.
25. W. Ley, *Your Life in 1977*, 1952.
26. O. Béliard, 'La Journée d'un parisien au XXIe siècle', *Lectures pour tous*, Dec. 1910, 291.

Chapter 1
1. 'Les Découvertes de demain', *Je sais tout*, 15 Mar. 1906, 193.
2. Ley.
3. I. Asimov, *Caves of Steel*. London, 1953, 23.
4. F. Pohl and C. M. Kornbluth, *The Space Merchants* (1952). Wendover, 1984, 3.
5. H. G. Wells, *When the Sleeper Wakes*. New York and London, 1899.
6. F. Leiber, *A Bad Day for Sales*, 1954.
7. Bester, 15.
8. J. Petithuguenin, 'Une mission dans la Lune', *Le Journal des voyages*, 1926, nos. 62 to 72, 1107.
9. I. Asimov, *Foundation* (1951). London, 1960, 13.
10. J. Verne, 'Une ville idéale [Amiens en l'an 2000]', *Mémoires de l'Académie des sciences, des lettres et des arts d'Amiens*, 1875, 354.
11. P. Anderson, *The Helping Hand*, 1950.
12. J. Verne, 'Au XXIXe siècle. La journée d'un journaliste américain en 2889', ('In the Year 2889', *The Forum*, New York, Feb. 1889. vol. VI, 664).
13. Atkins, 175-176
14. H. Allorge, *Le Grand Cataclysme: roman du centième siècle*. Paris, 1922, 19.
15. I. Asimov, *Nine Tomorrows* (1959). London, 1986, 50, 96.
16. R. Bradbury, *Fahrenheit 451*. London, 1957, 24.
17. I. Asimov, *Foundation*, 13.
18. J. Verne, *Amiens*. 352.
19. *Actuel*, op. cit., 20.
20. 'Les Découvertes de demain', 187-196.
21. R. Bradbury, *Fahrenheit 451*, 14.
22. Santos-Dumont, 'Ce que je ferai, ce que l'on fera', *Je sais tout*, 15 Feb. 1905, 109.
23. I. Asimov, *The Caves of Steel*. 191
24. P. F. Nowlan, *Armageddon 2419 AD* (1928). St Albans, 1976, 19.
25. Byrrh, '24 Regards sur l'avenir', a series of publicity images for Byrrh, 1943.
26. J. Verne, 'Au XXIXe siècle', 244.
27. Pohl & Kornbluth, 183.
28. 'Les Découvertes de demain', 193.
29. H. Kuttner and C. Moore, *The Twonky*, 1942.
30. M. Leinster, *A Logic Named Joe*, 1946.
31. 'Les Découvertes de demain', 188.
32. S. Gouchtchev and M. Vassiliev, *La vie au XXIe siècle*. Paris, 1964, 130.
33. Gouchtchev, 90.
34. Yefremov, 303.
35. C. Smith, *Alpha Ralpha Boulevard*, 1961.

36. Béliard, 'La Journée', 286.
37. 'La Maison rationelle', *Meccano Magazine*, no. 7, 1958, 15.
38. Kuttner and Moore, *Vintage Season*.
39. Pohl and Kornbluth, 5.
40. R. Bradbury, *The Martian Chronicles*. London, 1980, 20.
41. A Clarke, *Profiles of the Future*. London, 1964.
42. Atkins, 180.
43. 'Les Découvertes de demain', 193.
44. Allorge, 14-15.
45. D. de Chousy, 'Ignis', *La Science illustrée*. Paris, 1886, vols. XVII-XVIII, 93.

Chapter 2
1. 'Des usines qui marchent toutes seules', *Lectures pour tous*, 1 Mar. 1914, 983.
2. Byrrh.
3. Chousy, 77.
4. Béliard, 'La Journée', 290.
5. *Actuel*, op. cit.
6. C. Richet, 'Dans cent ans', *Revue scientifique*, 12 Mar. 1892, vol. XLVIII, 323.
7. René Barjavel, *Ravage*. Paris, 1943, 71.
8. Yefremov, 43.
9. Nowlan, 26.
10. Clarke, *Profiles of the Future*, 143.
11. Byrrh.
12. S. Lem, *The Twenty-Fourth Voyage*, 1957.
13. O. Béliard, 'Les Merveilles de l'ile mysterieuse', *Lectures pour tous*, Sept. 1911, 1072-1074.
14. E. M. Forster, 'The Machine Stops', 1909.
15. M. Leinster, *A Logic Named Joe*, 1946.
16. Allorge, 2.
17. Gouchtchev, 185.
18. Atkins, 148.
19. E. H. Weiss, 'L'Avenir de l'aviation' *Le Journal des voyages*, 1926, no. 65, 29 July, and no. 69, 26 Aug., 1229.
20. Chousy, 125.
21. Nowlan, 37.
22. *Amazing Stories*, back cover, Dec. 1944.
23. 'Les Féeries de l'avenir', *Lectures pour tous*, special issue, Dec. 1932, 49.
24. L. Del Rey, *And It Comes Out There*, 1953.
25. *Toute la radio*, no. 234, March-April 1959, 113.
26. R. Heinlein, 'By His Bootstraps', *Astounding Science Fiction*, Oct. 1941.
27. 'XXXe siècle', *Le Miroir du Monde*, special issue, 9 Dec. 1933, 52.
28. *Toute la radio*, op. cit., 113.
29. N. R. Jones, *The Planet of the Double Sun*, 1932.
30. M. Leinster, 'First Contact', *Astounding Science Fiction*, May 1945.
31. Yefremov, 91.
32. A. Clarke, 'Inside the Comet', *The Magazine of Fantasy and Science Fiction*, Oct. 1960.
33. Yefremov, 65.
34. Th. Moreux, 'Mars va nous parler', *Le Journal des voyages*, no. 2, 23 Oct. 1924 to no. 22, 12 Mar. 1925, 84.
35. 'Les Découvertes de demain', 89.
36. R. Zelazny, *Devil Car*, 1956.
37. C. D. Simak, 'Skirmish' (1950), *Science Fiction Thinking Machines*. New York, 1954.
38. S. Lem, 'The Story of the Calculator that Fought the Dragon', 1963.
39. D. Knight, *A for Anything*. London, 1961.
40. Clarke, *Profiles of the Future*, 198-199.
41. H. Harrison, *Portrait of the Artist*, 1964.
42. Asimov, *Nine Tomorrows*.

43. C. Smith, *Alpha Ralpha Boulevard*, 1961.
44. A. Clarke, 'Nine Billion Names of God',
New York, 1953.
45. Wolfe, 105.
46. *Le Miroir du monde*, op. cit., 20.
47. A. Saint-Ogan, *Zig et Puce au xxɪᵉ siècle*.
Paris, 1935.
48. Yefremov, 125.
49. Harrison, *Portrait of the Artist*.
50. L. Del Rey, 'Helen O'Loy', *Astounding
Science Fiction*, Dec. 1938
51 Simak, *City*.
52 Clarke, *Profiles of the Future*, 215.
53 Asimov, *I, Robot* (1950).
London, 1968.

Chapter 3
1. Wells, *When the Sleeper Wakes*.
2. Béliard, 'La Journée', 288.
3. H. G. Wells, *A Story of the Days to Come* (1899).
London, 1976.
4. Calvet, 324.
5. H. G. Wells, *A Story of the Days to Come*.
6. *Amazing Stories*, back cover, Aug. 1942.
7. Gouchtchev, 181.
8. Asimov, *The Caves of Steel*, 17.
9. A., Huxley, *Brave New World* (1932).
Harmondsworth, 1955, 58.
10. *Amazing Stories*, back cover, Apr. 1942.
11. H. Ferriss, exhibition catalogue for 'La Métropole du futur', C.C.I., Centre Georges Pompidou, Paris, 8 July-28 Sept. 1987, 169.
12. J. Blish, *The Seedling Stars*. London,1957, 42.
13. Ferriss, 169.
14. T. Moilin, *Paris en l'an 2000*. Paris, 1869, 78.
15. W. G. West, 'The Last Man', *Amazing Stories*, 1929.
16. A. France, *Sur la pierre blanche*.
Paris, 1924, 192-193.
17. G. Orwell, *1984* (1949).
Harmondsworth, 1984, 6.
18. Asimov, *Foundation*, 17.
19. F. Flagg, 'The Cities of Ardathia',
Amazing Stories, Mar. 1932.
20. West.
21. Flagg.
22. E. Smith, *A Day in the Suburbs*, 1960.
23. E. Zamyatin, *We*. London, 1970, 114.
24. Ley.
25. Wolfe, 96.
19. Wells, 'A Modern Utopia', 217.
27. Nowlan, 38-39.
28. Asimov, *The Caves of Steel*, 23.
29. West.
30. Asimov, *Foundation*, 19.
31. Yefremov, 285.
32. A. E. Van Vogt, *Slan* (1940).
London, 1960, 9.
33. Allorge, 9.
34. L. Claretie, *Paris depuis ses origines jusqu'en l'an 3000*. Paris, 1886, 341.
35. Bradbury, *The Martian Chronicles*, 190.
36. Weiss, 1150.
37. Nowlan, 56.

Chapter 4
1. Orwell.
2. Barjavel, 90.
3. E. Smith.

4. Orwell.
5. E. B. Corbett, *New Amazonia:
a Foretaste of the Future*.
London, 1889.
6. Allorge, 43.
7. 'Le Crapouillot en l'an 3000',
Le Crapouillot, special issue,
Christmas 1919, 191, 5.
8. Kuttner and Moore, *Vintage Season*.
9. Kuttner and Moore, *The Twonky*, 1942.
10. Verne, 'La Journée d'un journaliste', 670.
11. E. B.,Wertenbaker, 'The Coming of the Ice Age',
Amazing Stories, June 1926.
12. Nowlan, 15-16.
13. Bester, 145.
14. Atkins, 119-120.
15. Bester, 86.
16. Asimov, *The Caves of Steel*, 21.
17. D. Knight, 'To Serve Man',
Galaxy Science Fiction, Nov. 1950.
18. Wolfe, 18
19. Russell, in Atkins, 107.
20. P. K. Dick, 'The Father Thing',
The Magazine of Fantasy and Science Fiction,
Dec. 1954.
21. Adornier, 75.
22. Bradbury, *Fahrenheit 451*.
23. Wertenbaker.
24. Orwell, 313.
25. Bradbury, *The Martian Chronicles*.
26. *Toute la radio*, op. cit., 114.
27. Pohl and Kornbluth, 5.
28. Bradbury, *Fahrenheit 451*, 48.
29. Zamyatin, 52.
30. Atkins, 174.
31. L. Daudet, *Le Napus, fléau de l'an 2227*.
Paris, 1927, x.
32. M. Heimer, *Surhommes et surmondes*.
Paris, 1961, 182-183.
33. Huxley, 17.
34. Orwell, 263.
35. West.
36. Orwell, 273.
37. Gheoghiou, in Atkins, 42-43.
38. Kuttner and Moore, *The Twonky*.
39. Zamyatin, 23.
40. Kuttner and Moore, *Vintage Season*.
41. Bester, 97.
42. Wertenbaker.
43. Bester, 190.
44. West.
45. Huxley, 22.
46. Heimer, 89.
47. France, 220.
48. Atkins, 20.

Chapter 5
1. Béliard, 'La Journée', 291.
2. Petithuguenin, 107.
3. J. H. Rosny, *La Mort de la Terre*, (1910).
Paris: Denoel, 1983, p. 9.
4. 'Alerte à bord de la fusée Terre-Lune',
Meccano Magazine, no. 2, 1958, 14.
5. Bradbury, *The Martian Chronicles*, 16
6. Clarke, *Profiles of the Future*.
7. Pohl and Kornbluth, 21.
8. Pohl and Kornbluth, 6.
9. Asimov, *Nine Tomorrows*, 130.

10. R. Heinlein, 'Skylift', *Imagination*, Nov. 1953.
11. Asimov, *Foundation*, 10.
12. Asimov, *Nine Tomorrows*, 94.
13. Wells, *The First Men in the Moon*, 316.
14. Rosny, 33.
15. Rosny, 16-17.
16. S. Lem, *Solaris*, (1961). London, 1971, 171.
17. H. Harrison, *A Final Encounter*, 1964.
18. Bradbury, *The Martian Chronicles*, 76.
19. P. Anderson, *The Helping Hand*, 1950.
20. D. A. Stuart, 'Cloak of Aesir', *Astounding
Science Fiction*, 1939.
21. Asimov, *The Caves of Steel*, 60.
22. C.D. Simak, 'Rim of the Deep', *Astounding
Science Fiction*, May 1940.
23. Van Vogt, 89.
24. Blish, 43.
25. Pohl and Kornbluth, 163.
26. Clarke, *Profiles of the Future*.
27. Clarke, *Profiles of the Future*, 94.
28. P. Phillips, *University*, 1954.
29. J. Williams, *Gifts of the Gods*, 1962.
30. Henriot, 6.
31. 'Une exploration polaire aux ruines de Paris',
Lectures pour tous, June 1911, 799.
32. Allorge, 31.
33. Wells, *The War of the Worlds*, 827.
34. Jones.
35. L. Del Rey, *The Last Earthman*, 1965.
36. C. Flammarion, 'La Fin du monde',
Je sais tout, 15 Feb. 1905, 53-62.
37. P. Boulle, *La Planète des singes*,
Paris, 1963, 166-167.
38. E. Haraucourt, 'La Fin du monde', *L'Effort*.
Paris, 1894, 99.
39. Rosny, 104.
40. A. Conan Doyle, *The Poison Belt*.
London, 1913, 82.
41. Flammarion, 58.
42. Rosny, 136.
43. W. O. Stapledon, *Last and First Men*.
New York, 1930.
44. L. Del Rey, *Instinct*, 1951.
45. Del Rey, *The Last Earthman*.
46. Yefremov, 206.
47. Simak, *City*, 8.
48. Wertenbaker.
49. Rosny, 220.
50. J. Spitz, *Les Évadés de l'an 4000*.
Paris, 1936, 217.
51. Asimov, *Foundation*, 34.
52. J. Verne, 'L'Éternel Adam',
*Hier et demain :
contes et nouvelles*.
Paris, 1910, 253.
53. Clarke, *Profiles of the Future*, 114
54. Clarke, *Profiles of the Future*, 118.
55. Gouchtchev, 245
56. Wertenbaker.
57. Leinster, 'First Contact'.
58. J. Vance, 'The Moon Moth',
Galaxy Science Fiction, Aug. 1961.
59. Blish, 8.
60. Simak, *City*.
61. West.
62. Yefremov, 69.
63. Atkins, 186-1877.
64. Yefremov, 206.

WORKS CITED

Actuel Kyrou (Ariel), 'Vive l'an 2 000 : ses avions sans pilote et ses briquets atomiques', *Actuel, 50 idées-100 livres qui ont frappé le monde*, special issue, April 1989.

Adornier Adornier (Pierre), *La Mort du film* (1926), in *Ailleurs et demain a vingt ans*. Paris: R. Laffont, 1990.

Allorge Allorge (Henri), *Le Grand cataclysme : roman du centième siècle*. Paris: G. Crès, 1922.

Anderson Anderson (Poul) 'The Guardians of Time', in *The Magazine of Fantasy and Science Fiction*, 1954.
Anderson (Poul), *The Helping Hand*. Street and Smith, 1950.

Asimov Asimov (Isaac), *Foundation* (1951). London: Panther, 1960.
Asimov (Isaac), *I Robot* (1950). London: Panther, 1968.
Asimov (Isaac), *Nine Tomorrows* (1959). London: Grafton Collins, 1986.
Asimov (Isaac), *The Caves of Steel*. London: Boardman, 1954.

Atkins Atkins (John), *Tomorrow Revealed*. London: Neville Spearman, 1955.

Barjavel Barjavel (René), *Ravage*. Paris: Denoël, 1943.

Béliard Béliard (Octave), 'La journée d'un Parisien au xxie siècle', *Lectures pour tous*, December 1910, pp. 286-296.
Béliard (Octave), 'Les merveilles de l'île mystérieuse', *Lectures pour tous*, September 1911, pp. 1067-1078.

Bester Bester (Alfred), *The Demolished Man* (1952). Harmondsworth: Penguin, 1979.

Blish Blish (James), *The Seedling Stars*. London: Faber and Faber, 1957.

Boulle Boulle (Pierre), *La Planète des singes*. Paris: R. Julliard, 1963.

Bradbury Bradbury (Ray), *Fahrenheit 451* (1950). London: Corgi, 1957.
Bradbury (Ray), *The Martian Chronicles* (1951). London: Granada, 1980.

Byrrh 24 Regards sur l'avenir, a series of advertising images for Byrrh (1943).

Calvet Calvet (Émile), 'Dans mille ans', in *Le Musée des familles*, 1883.

Chousy Chousy (Didier de), 'Ignis', in *La Science illustrée*, vol. XVII-XVIII, 1896.

Claretie Claretie (Léo), *Paris depuis ses origines jusqu'en l'an 3000*. Paris: Charavay Frères, 1886.

Clarke Clarke (Arthur C.), 'Inside the Comet', in *The Magazine of Fantasy and Science Fiction*, October 1960.
Clarke (Arthur C.), 'The Nine Billion Names of God', in *Star Science Fiction Stories*, ed. F. Pohl. New York: Ballantine, 1953.
Clarke (Arthur C.), *Profiles of the Future* (1962). London: Pan, 1964.

Conan Doyle Conan Doyle (Arthur), *The Poison Belt*. London: Hodder and Stoughton, 1913.

Corbett Corbett (E. B.), *New Amazonia : a Foretaste of the Future*. London: Lambert, 1889.

Le Crapouillot 'Le Crapouillot en l'an 3000', *Le Crapouillot*, special issue, Christmas 1919.

Danrit Danrit (Capitain), *L'Invasion noire : la guerre au xxe siècle*, 3 vols. Paris: E. Flammarion, 1919.

Daudet Daudet (Léon), *Le Napus, fléau de l'an 2227*. Paris: Flammarion, 1927.

Del Rey Del Rey (Lester), *And It Comes Out There*. Vanguard, 1953.
Del Rey (Lester), 'Helen O'Loy', in *Astounding Science Fiction*, December 1938.
Del Rey (Lester), *Instinct*. Street and Smith, 1951.
Del Rey (Lester), *The Last Earthman*. Galaxy Publishing Corp., 1965.

Dick Dick (Philip K.), 'The Father Thing', in *The Magazine of Fantasy and Science Fiction*, December 1954.

Ferréol Ferréol (Pierre), *La Prise de Londres au xxe siècle*. Paris: L. Boulanger, 1891.

Ferriss Ferriss (Hugh), exhibition catalogue for 'La Métropole du futur', 8 July-28 September 1987, the Centre de Création Industrielle, Centre Georges Pompidou, Paris.

Flagg Flagg (Francis), 'The Cities of Ardathia', in *Amazing Stories*, March 1932.

Flammarion Flammarion (Camille), 'La Fin du monde', in *Je sais tout*, 15 February 1905, pp. 53-62.

Forster Forster (Edward Morgan), 'The Machine Stops' (1909), in *The Collected Short Stories of E. M. Forster*. London: Sidgewick and Jackson, 1954.

France France (Anatole), *Sur la pierre blanche*. Paris: La Connaissance, 1924.

Gouchtchev Gouchtchev (Sergey) and Vassiliev (Mikhaïl), *La Vie au xxe siècle* (1959). Paris: Buchet-Chastel, 1964.

Haraucourt Haraucourt (Edmond), 'La Fin du monde', in *L'Effort*. Paris: Académie des Beaux Livres Bibliophiles Contemporains, 1894.

Harrison Harrison (Harry), *A Portrait of the Artist*. Mercury Press, 1964.
Harrison (Harry), *A Final Encounter*. Galaxy Publishing Corp., 1964.

Heimer Heimer (Marc), *Surhommes et Surmondes*. Paris: Julliard, 1961.

Heinlein Heinlein (Robert), 'By his Bootstraps', in *Astounding Science Fiction*, October 1941.
Heinlein (Robert), 'Sky Lift', in *Imagination*, November 1953.

Henriot Maigriot (Henry), a.k.a. Henriot, *Paris en l'an 3000*. Paris: H. Laurens, 1912.

Huxley Huxley (Aldous), *Brave New World*. Harmondsworth: Penguin, 1932.

Ivoi Ivoi (Paul d') and Royet (Colonel), *La Patrie en danger : histoire de la guerre future*. Paris: H. Geffroy, 1904.

Je Sais Tout 'Les découvertes de demain', *Je sais tout*, 15 March 1905, pp.187-196.

Jones Jones (Neil R.), *Planet of the Double Sun*. 1932.

Knight Knight (Damon), *A for Anything* (1957). London: Four Square, 1961.
Knight (Damon), 'Auto-da-fé', in *Galaxy Science Fiction*, February 1961.
Knight (Damon), 'To Serve Man', in *Galaxy Science Fiction*, November 1950.

Kuttner and Moore Kuttner (Henry) and Moore (Catherine L.), *Vintage Season*.
Kuttner (Henry) and Moore (Catherine L.), *The Twonky*, 1942.

Lectures Pour Tous 'Une exploration polaire aux ruines de Paris', *Lectures pour tous*, June 1911, pp. 797-808.
'Les Féeries de l'avenir', *Lectures pour tous*, special issue, December 1932.
'Dans la nuit à travers les airs', *Lectures pour tous*, 15 February 1914, pp. 915-918.
'Les transatlantiques de l'air', *Lectures pour tous*, 1 November 1913, pp. 253-263.
'Des usines qui marchent toutes seules', *Lectures pour tous*, 1 March 1914, pp. 983-990.

Leiber Leiber (Fritz), *A Bad Day for Sales*, 1954.

Leinster Leinster (Murray), *A Logic Named Joe*. Street and Smith, 1946.
Leinster (Murray), 'First Contact', in *Astounding Science Fiction*, May 1945.

Lem Lem (Stanislas), *Solaris* (1961). London: Faber and Faber, 1971.
Lem (Stanislas), 'The Story of the Calculator that Fought the Dragon' (1963), in *Other Worlds, Other Seas*, anthology, Suvin Darko, ed. New York: Random House, 1970.
Lem (Stanislas), 'The Twenty-Fourth Voyage', 1957.

Ley Ley (Willy), *Your Life in 1977*, 1952.

Maurois Maurois (André), *Deux fragments d'une histoire universelle, 1992 : fragments d'une histoire universelle générale publiée par l'Université de Tombouctou*. Paris: Éd. des Portiques, 1928.

Meccano Magazine 'Alerte à bord de la fusée Terre-Lune', *Meccano Magazine*, no. 2, 1958.
'La Maison rationnelle', *Meccano Magazine*, no. 7, 1958.

Miroir du Monde 'xxxe siècle', *Le Miroir du Monde*, special issue, 9 December 1933.

Moilin Moilin (Tony), *Paris en l'an 2000*. Paris: the author and Librairie de la Renaissance, 1869.

Montorgueil Montorgueil (Georges), 'Au pays des prophètes : Ce que serait la société de demain', *Je sais tout*, 15 Oct. 1906, pp. 279-286.

Moreux Moreux (Th.), 'Mars va nous parler', *Le journal des voyages*, no.2, 23 October 1924 to no. 22, 12 March 1925.

Nowlan Nowlan (Philip Francis), *Armageddon 2419 A.D.* (1928).
St Albans: Panther, 1976.

Orwell Orwell (George), *1984* (1949). Harmondsworth: Penguin, 1984.

Petithuguenin Petithuguenin (Jean), 'Une mission dans la Lune', *Le Journal des voyages,* 1926, nos. 62 to 72.

Phillips Phillips (Peter), *University.* Gold and Crown, 1954.

Pohl and Kornbluth Pohl (Frederick) and Kornbluth (Cyril M.),
The Space Merchants (1952). Wendover: John Fairchild, 1984.

Punch *Cap and Bell : Punch's Chronicle of English History in the Making.* London: Macdonald, 1972.

Toute la Radio *Toute la radio,* no. 234, March-April 1959.

Richet Richet (Charles), 'Dans cent ans', *Revue scientifique,*
12 December 1891, vol. XLVIII, pp. 737-747 ; 19 December 1891,
pp. 779-785, vol. XLIX; 30 January 1892, pp. 135-144 ;
12 March 1892, pp. 321-332.

Robida Robida (Albert), *La Guerre au xxᵉ siècle*, in Béraldi (Henri),
Un caricaturiste prophète. Paris: Dorbon aîné, 1916.
Robida (Albert), *Le vingtième siècle,* new ed. Paris: G. Decaux, 1884.

Rosny Rosny (J. H.), *La Mort de la Terre,* (1910). Paris: Denoël, 1983.

Rostand Rostand (Jean), Pensées d'un biologiste (1954). Paris: Stock, 1978.

Saint-Ogan Saint-Ogan (Alain), *Zig et Puce au xxiᵉ siècle.* Paris:
Hachette, 1935.

Santos-Dumont 'Ce que je ferai, ce que l'on fera', *Je sais tout,* 15 February 1905.

Science et vie *Science et vie junior,* no. 32, December 1991.

Simak Simak (Clifford D.), *City.* London: Weidenfeld and Nicholson, 1952.
Simak (Clifford D.), 'Rim of the Deep', in *Astounding Science Fiction,* May 1940.
Simak (Clifford D.), 'Skirmish' (1950), in *Science Fiction Thinking Machines.* New York: Vanguard Press, 1954.

Smith, C. Smith (Cordwainer), *Alpha Ralpha Boulevard,* 1961.

Smith, E. Smith (Evelyn E.), *A Day in the Suburbs,* 1960.

Spitz Spitz (Jacques), *Les Évadés de l'an 4000.* Paris: Gallimard, 1936.

Stapledon Stapledon (William Olaf), *Last and First Men.*
New York: Methuen, 1930.

Stuart Stuart (Don A.), 'Cloak of Aesir', in *Astounding Science Fiction,* 1939.

Sturgeon Sturgeon (Theodore), 'The Golden Egg', in *Unknown,* August 1941.

Van Vogt Van Vogt (A. E.), *Slan.* London: Panther, 1940.

Vance Vance (Jack), 'The Moon Moth', in *Galaxy Science Fiction,* August 1961.

Verne Verne (Jules), 'Une ville idéale [Amiens en l'an 2000]', in *Mémoires de l'Académie des sciences, des lettres et des arts d'Amiens,* 1875, pp. 347-378.
Verne (Jules), 'L'éternel Adam', *Hier et demain : contes et nouvelles.* Paris: Hetzel, 1910.
Verne (Jules), 'Au xxixᵉ siècle. La journée d'un journaliste américain en 2889', *Hier et demain : contes et nouvelles.* Paris: Hetzel, 1910 [first appeared in English as 'In the Year 2889' in *The Forum,* February 1889. New York: Forum Publishing Co., vol. vi.].

Weiss Weiss (E. H.), 'L'avenir de l'aviation', *Le Journal des voyages,* 1926, no. 65, 29 July 1926 and no. 69, 26 August 1926.

Wells Wells (Herbert George), *The First Men in the Moon.*
London: George Noones, 1901.
Wells (Herbert George), *The Island of Dr. Moreau.*
London: Heineman, 1896.
Wells (Herbert George), 'A Modern Utopia' (1905),
in *The Works of H.G. Wells.* London: Fisher Unwin, 1925, vol. ix.
Wells (Herbert George), *A Story of the Days to Come* (1899).
London: Corgi, 1979.
Wells (Herbert George), *The War of the Worlds.*
London: Heineman, 1898.
Wells (Herbert George), *When the Sleeper Wakes.*
New York and London: Harper, 1899.

Wertenbaker Wertenbaker (G. Peyton), 'The Coming of the Ice Age',
in *Amazing Stories,* June 1926.

West West (Wallace G.), 'The Last Man', in *Amazing Stories,* 1929.

Williams Williams (Jay), *Gifts of the Gods,* 1962.

Wolfe Wolfe (Bernard), *Limbo* (1954). Harmondsworth: Penguin, 1961.

Yefremov Yefremov (Ivan), *Andromeda, A Space-Age Tale.* Moscow:
Foreign Language Publishing House, 1960.

Zamyatin Zamyatin (E.), *We.* London: Jonathan Cape, 1970.

Zelazny Zelazny (Roger), *Devil Car.* Galaxy Publishing Corp., 1956.

LIST OF ILLUSTRATIONS

Frontispiece: Frank R. Paul, 'The Man from Mars', in *Fantastic Adventures,* 1939 (detail of illustration 27, chap. 5).

Title page: Bus, 'Aviation of the 21st Century', *Judge,* 1911 (illustration 29, chap. 4).

Preface

Still from *The Misadventures of Merlin Jones,* a Walt Disney production, United States, 1933. Photo Édimédia, Paris.

Introduction: The Future As History

1. Still from *Le Voyage dans la Lune,* directed by Georges Méliès, France, 1902. Photo Collection La Cinémathèque Française, Paris. © SPADEM 1993.

2. James Leech, *Hyde Park As It Will Be,* tinted etching, London, *c.*1820. La Maison d'ailleurs, Yverdon-les-Bains. Photo Flammarion.

3. Illustration for Savinien de Cyrano de Bergerac's *Voyage aux états et empires du Soleil,* Amsterdam, 1699. Cabinet des Estampes (Ib mat 1), Bibliothèque Nationale, Paris. Photo B. N.

4. L. Vallet, illustration for *Aventures extraordinaires d'un savant russe,* by Georges Le Faure et Henri de Graffigny, Paris, 1889. Cabinet des Estampes (Tb 774), Bibliothèque Nationale, Paris. Photo B. N.

5. Henri de Montaut 'Les trains de projectiles pour la lune', illustration for *De la Terre à la Lune,* by Jules Verne. Paris: J. Hetzel, 1868. Photo Jean Loup Charmet, Paris.

6. Travelators at the Exposition Universelle, Paris, 1900. Cabinet des Estampes (Ve 605), Bibliothèque Nationale, Paris. Photo B. N.

7. Lewis Baumer,'Wireless Telegraphy, Scene in Hyde Park', *Punch,* 1906. Cabinet des Estampes (Tf 667), Bibliothèque Nationale, Paris. Photo B. N.

8. 'Frank Reade Jr and his New Electric Air Ship', front cover illustration for *Eclipse.* New York, 1892. Photo Mary Evans Picture Library, London.

9. Jules Beau, *Flying Machine with Monsieur Villard at the Controls,* photograph, 1901. Cabinet des Estampes (Kg 37 vol. 16), Bibliothèque Nationale, Paris. Photo B. N.

10. Grandville, 'Le Pouce', illustration for *Un autre monde.* Paris: H. Fournier, 1844. Cabinet des Estampes (Tf 99b), Bibliothèque Nationale, Paris. Photo B. N.

11. Max Ernst, *La Femme 100 Têtes.* Paris: Éd. du Carrefour, 1929. Cabinet des Estampes (Tf 296), Bibliothèque Nationale, Paris. Photo B. N.

12. 'La Guerre de demain', colour postcard, *c.*1910. Private Collection. All rights reserved.

13. Orlando, Ford Gemini, the 'two-seater' of the future. 1965, 'Almanac of the 80s', special issue of *Actuel,* 1979. All rights reserved.

14. Still from *Modern Times,* directed by Charlie Chaplin, United States, 1936. Photo PROD/DB.

15. Grandville 'Concert à la vapeur', illustration for *Un autre monde,* Paris: H. Fournier, 1844. Cabinet des Estampes (Tf 99b), Bibliothèque Nationale, Paris. Photo B. N.

16. William Heath Robinson, 'An interesting and elegant apparatus designed to overcome once and for all the difficulties of conveying green peas to the mouth', magazine illustration, London *c.*1920. Photo Mary Evans Picture Library, London.

17. Vladimir Tatlin, Model for the *Monument to the Third International,* 1919. Photo Bildarchiv Preussischer Kulturbesitz, Berlin.

18. Scene from the play *RUR* by Karel Capek. London: Doubleday, Page & Co., 1923. Photo Mander & Mitchenson, Beckenham (Kent).

19. Still from *The First Men in the Moon,* directed by Nathan Juran, Great Britain, 1964, based on the novel by H. G. Wells. Photo Édimédia, Paris.

20. Etienne Louis Boullée, *Coupe du Cénotaphe à Newton, effect de jour,* ink and watercolour, 1784. Cabinet des Estampes (Ha 57), Bibliothèque Nationale, Paris. Photo B. N.

21. Tony Garnier, Ironworks, view of the blast furnaces, design for *Une Cité Industrielle,* pen and watercolour, 1917. Musée des Beaux-Arts, Lyon. Photo Studio Basset.

22. Still from *Aelita,* directed by Yakov Protozanov, U.S.S.R., 1924, based on the novel by Alexei Tolstoy. Photo Collection La Cinémathèque Française, Paris.

23. Le Corbusier, aerial perspective of the project for a central station flanked by four skyscrapers, for the *Plan Voisin,* ink drawing, 1925. Fondation Le Corbusier, Paris. © SPADEM, 1993.

24. Henri Cartier-Bresson, *Expo '67,* Montreal, photograph, 1967. H. Cartier-Bresson/Magnum, Paris.

25. Kisho Kurokawa, *Helix City,* urban planning project for Tokyo, ink drawing, 1961. Private collection. All rights reserved.

Chapter 0

1. *Saturday Night 1980,* 1958, 'Almanac of the 80s', special issue of *Actuel,* 1979. Photo all rights reserved.

2. Fred T. Jane, illustration for *Hartmann the Anarchist,* by Douglas Fawcett, London, 1896. Photo Mary Evans Picture Library, London.

3. Paul de Sémant, illustration for *L'Invasion noire,* by Capitaine Danrit, Paris, 1919. Département des Imprimés (8° Y^2 60371), Bibliothèque Nationale, Paris. Photo B. N.

4. Henri Lanos, 'La Guerre future', illustration for 'l'Automobile, reine du monde', *Je sais tout,* 15 March 1906. Départment des Imprimés (8°Z 17063), Bibliothèque Nationale, Paris. Photo B. N.

5. Albert Robida, 'La Guerre au vingtième siècle', *La Caricature,* 27 October 1883. Photo Tapabor.

6. 'High-Life Taylor', advertisement, 1912. Recueils (4°Z 3896), Bibliothèque Nationale, Paris. Photo B. N.

7. 'L'Europe de demain', *L'Illustration,* 23 January 1909. Département des Imprimés (Fol. Lc^2 1549), Bibliothèque Nationale, Paris. Photo B. N.

8. Albert Robida, 'Station d'aérocabs de la Tour Saint-Jacques', illustration for *Le Vingtième siècle.* Paris: G. Decaux, 1883. Photo Flammarion.

9. Albert Robida, 'Petite maison de campagne', illustration for *Le Vingtième siècle.* Paris: G. Decaux, 1883. Département des Imprimés (4°Y2 5005), Bibliothèque Nationale, Paris. Photo B. N.

10. Henri Lanos, 'Le Train monorail et aérien', illustration for 'Les découvertes de demain', *Je sais tout,* 15 February 1905. Département des Imprimés (8°Z 17063), Bibliothèque Nationale, Paris. Photo B. N.

11. Albert Robida, 'Le Théâtre chez soi par le téléphonoscope', illustration for *Le Vingtième siècle.* Paris: G. Decaux, 1883. All rights reserved.

12. Henri Lanos, 'Notre-Dame gare aérienne', illustration for 'Ce que je ferai ce que l'on fera', by Santos-Dumont, *Je sais tout,* 15 February 1905. Département des Imprimés (8°Z 17063 p. 107), Bibliothèque Nationale, Paris. Photo B. N.

13. Still from *1984,* directed by Michael Anderson, Great Britain, 1955, based on the novel by George Orwell. Photo Collection La Cinémathèque Française.

14. Damblans, 'Les Atmophites', illustration for 'Ignis', by Didier de Chousy in *La Science illustrée,* no. 450, 1896. Département des Imprimés (4°R 767 p. 93), Bibliothèque Nationale, Paris. Photo B. N.

15. Albert Robida, 'Paris la nuit', illustration for *Le Vingtième siècle.* Paris: G. Decaux, 1883. All rights reserved.

16. Albert Robida, 'Modes parisiennes en 1952', illustration for *Le Vingtième siècle.* Paris: G. Decaux, 1883. All rights reserved.

17. Albert Robida, 'Un quartier embrouillé', illustration for *La Vie électrique.* Paris: G. Decaux, 1890. Département des Imprimés (4°Y^2 5065 p. 128), Bibliothèque Nationale, Paris. Photo B. N.

18. Albert Robida, 'La Lune rapprochée', illustration for *Le Vingtième siècle,* Paris: G. Decaux, 1883. Photo Jean Loup Charmet, Paris.

19. Albert Robida, 'Gare du Tube du Sud à Paris', illustration for *Le Vingtième siècle.* Paris: G. Decaux, 1883. Bibliothèque des Arts Decoratifs, Paris. Photo Jean Loup Charmet, Paris.

Chapter 1

1. Still from *Just Imagine,* directed by David Butler, United States, 1930. Photo PROD/DB.

2. H. Furniss, *Shaving in the electrical home,* 1885. Photo Mary Evans Picture Library, London.

3. Henri Lanos, 'Le Règne de la machine', illustration for 'Ce que serait la société de demain', by Georges Montorgueil, in *Je sais tout,* 15 October 1906. Département des Imprimés (8°Z 17063 p. 283), Bibliothèque Nationale, Paris. Photo B. N.

4. *En l'an 2000,* publicity cards for Vieillemard printing firm, 1910. Cabinet des Estampes (Ib mat 2a), Bibliothèque Nationale, Paris. Photo B. N.

5. Albert Robida, 'La Sortie de l'Opéra en l'an 2000', *L'Album,* X, March 1902. Cabinet des Estampes (Tf 239 X), Bibliothèque Nationale, Paris. Photo B. N.

6. Joseph Hémard, illustration for *Nouveau code des impôts pour l'an fiscal 1995,* by Marcel Charpaux. Paris: Imprimerie E. Desfossés 1947. La Maison d'ailleurs, Yverdon-les-Bains. Photo Flammarion.

7. 'United Air Line Terminal', *Life,* 1910. Photo Michael Dyer Associates Ltd., London.

8. Illustration from 'La Maison sans domestiques', by C. M. Leneau in *Je sais tout,* 15 October 1924. Photo Édimédia, Paris.

9. Bertall, illustration for *Le Monde tel qu'il sera,* by Émile Souvestre, Paris: N. Coquebert,1845. Photo Édimédia, Paris.

10. 'En l'an 2012', publicity for Lombart chocolate. Imprimerie Norgeu, 1912. Cabinet des Estampes (Ib mat 2a), Bibliothèque Nationale, Paris. Photo B. N.

11. Alain Saint-Ogan, *Zig et Puce au* XXIe *siècle.* Paris: Hachette,1935. Cabinet des Estampes (Ka 404-10, 4°), Bibliothèque Nationale, Paris. Photo B. N.

12. Francis W. Dahl, illustration for *Dahl's Brave New World,* by Charles W. Morton. Boston, 1947. All rights reserved.

13. Francis W. Dahl, illustration for *Dahl's Boston,* by Charles W. Morton. Boston, 1946. Cabinet des Estampes (Tf 579, 4°), Bibliothèque Nationale, Paris. Photo B. N.

14. Frank R. Paul, illustration for 'Ralph 124C 41+', by Hugo Gernsback, *Amazing Stories Quarterly,* spring 1929. All rights reserved.

15. 'Suspended gravitation', cover for *Electrical Experimenter,* February *c.*1920. Private collection. All rights reserved.

16. Lucien Guy, Avion-caravane, *Fantasio,* November 1912. Photo Mary Evans Picture Library, London.

17. Frank R. Paul, illustration for 'Ralph 124C 41+', by Hugo Gernsback, *Amazing Stories Quarterly,* spring 1929

18. Guy Sabran, Traffic patterns of the future, magazine illustration, Paris, 1934. Photo Mary Evans Picture Library, London.

19. Leo Morey, illustration for 'Service first', by David H. Keller, *Amazing Stories Quarterly,* winter 1930. All rights reserved.

20. Walter Popp, cover illustration for *Startling Stories,* May 1953. La Maison d'ailleurs, Yverdon-les-Bains. Photo Flammarion.

21. Edmund A. Emshwiller, illustration for 'Milady's Boudoir', cover illustration for *Galaxy Science Fiction,* January 1955. Jacques Sadoul Collection. All rights reserved.

22. J. Touchet, Enlèvements en auto, *Lectures pour tous,* December 1932. Département des Imprimés (8°Z 14580). Bibliothèque Nationale, Paris. Photo B. N.

23. Frank R. Paul, illustration for 'A Story of the Days to Come', by H. G. Wells, *Amazing Stories,* April 1928. All rights reserved.

Chapter 2

1. Frank R. Paul, illustration for 'Into the Subconscious', by Ray Avery Myer, cover illustration for *Science Wonder Stories,* October 1929. Science Fiction Foundation, Essex. Photo Bernard Peek.

2. Henri Lanos, 'A Farm in 1950', *Je sais tout,* 15 March 1905. Département des Imprimés (8°Z17063 p. 221), Bibliothèque Nationale, Paris. Photo B. N.

3. Paul de Sémant, 'Colleuse automatique d'affiches', illustration for *L'Invasion noire,* by Danrit, Paris, 1919. Département des Imprimés (8°Y2 60371 p. 302). Bibliothèque Nationale, Paris. Photo B. N.

4. Ed Zier, illustration for 'La Dérive', by N. Balleygnier and L. Gasty, *L'Ouvrier,* 19 September 1891. La Maison d'ailleurs, Yverdon-les-Bains. Photo Flammarion.

5. Alex Schomburg, cover illustration for *Startling Stories,* April 1952. La Maison d'ailleurs, Yverdon-les-Bains. Photo Flammarion.

6. Paris-Londres en taxi-volant, cover illustration for *Meccano Magazine,* 1958, No. 3. All rights reserved.

7. 'Captation de l'électricité de l'atmosphère', publicity illustration for Byrrh, 1943. Cabinet des Estampes, Bibliothèque Nationale, Paris. Photo B. N.

8. 'Brantonne', cover for *Infernale menace,* by Vargo Statten. Paris: Éditions du Fleuve noir, 1953. La Maison d'ailleurs, Yverdon-les-Bains. Photo Flammarion.

9. 'Allo, allo, ici radio-Mars', *Lectures pour tous,* December 1932. Département des Imprimés (8°Z 14580) Bibliothèque Nationale, Paris. Photo B. N.

10. 'Le rapide du XXIe siècle', publicity image for Byrrh, 1943. Cabinet des Estampes, Bibliothèque Nationale, Paris. Photo B. N.

11. Frank R. Paul, illustration for 'The Skylark of Space', by E. E. Smith, cover, *Amazing Stories,* August 1928. All rights reserved.

12. Alain Saint-Ogan, *Zig et Puce au* XXIe *siècle.* Paris: Hachette, 1935. Cabinet des Estampes (Ka 404-10 4° p.11), Bibliothèque Nationale, Paris. Photo B. N.

13. Illustration for Armin Neufeld, *A Trencsén-Megyei-Verseny-Feltalalok* [The inventors of cuckoos in the Trencsen region]. Budapest, 1921. Photo Jean-Loup Charmet, Paris.

14. 'Old Age Rejuvenator Centrifuge', cover illustration for *Science and Mechanics,* 1935. Photo Mary Evans Picture Library, London.

15. Norman Saunders, illustration for 'Newscast', by Harl Vincent, cover illustration for Marvel Science Stories, April-May1939. Jacques Sadoul Collection. All rights reserved.

16. Robot Factory, *Super Science Stories,* November 1950. La Maison d'ailleurs, Yverdon-les-Bains. Photo Flammarion.

17. Frank R. Paul, illustration for 'The Onslaught from Venus', by Frank Phillips, cover illustration for *Science Wonder Stories,* September 1929. Photo Michael Dyer Associates Ltd., London.

18. Edmund A. Emswiller, cover illustration for *Rocket Stories,* April 1953. Jacques Sadoul Collection. All rights reserved.

19. Frank R. Paul, illustration for 'Misfit', by Michael Fischer, *Science Fiction Plus,* December 1953. La Maison d'ailleurs, Yverdon-les-Bains. Photo Flammarion.

20. Edmund A. Emswiller, illustration for 'The Man Who Was Six', by F. L. Wallace, cover illustration for *Galaxy Science Fiction,* September 1954. Jacques Sadoul Collection. All rights reserved.

21. Julian S. Krupa, illustration for 'Secret of the Buried City', by John Russell Fearn, *Amazing Stories,* May 1939. All rights reserved.

22. Charles Schneeman, illustration for 'The Mechanical Mice', *Astounding Science Fiction,* January 1941. Science Fiction Foundation, Essex. Photo Bernard Peek.

23. J. Ruger, illustration for *Scientific Detective Monthly,* March 1930. All rights reserved.

Chapter 3

1. Biedermann, Aerial Station, drawing, 1916. All rights reserved.

2. 'La détrônée', *Lectures pour tous,* December 1932. Département des Imprimés (8°Z 14580), Bibliothèque Nationale, Paris. Photo B. N.

3. Biron-Roger, 'Paris futur', *Lectures pour tous,* December 1910. Département des Imprimés (8°Z 14580), Bibliothèque Nationale, Paris. Photo B. N.

4. Cylindrical skyscraper with aerial station, publicity image for Byrrh, 1943. Cabinet des Estampes (Ib mat 2a), Bibliothèque Nationale, Paris. Photo B. N.

5. Woolley, *Town Planning,* 1920. Photo Mary Evans Picture Library, London.

6. Bettmann, Aerial City, c.1890. The Bettmann Archives. All rights reserved.

7. 'xxxe siècle', cover illustration for *Le Miroir du Monde,* Christmas 1933. Photo Tapabor, Paris.

8. Alain Saint-Ogan, *Zig et Puce au xxie siècle,* Paris: Hachette, 1935. Cabinet des Estampes (Ka 404-10 4° p. 13), Bibliothèque Nationale, Paris. Photo B. N.

9. Julian S. Krupa, 'Cities of Tomorrow', cover illustration for *Amazing Stories,* August 1939. Cabinet des Estampes (Tb 971, 4° p. 89), Bibliothèque Nationale, Paris. Photo B. N.

10. Frank R. Paul, illustration for Earl L. Bell, 'The Moon of Doom', *Amazing Stories Quarterly,* winter 1928. All rights reserved.

11. Hugh Ferriss, Aerial traffic patterns, charcoal drawing, *c.* 1926. Avery Architectural and Fine Arts Library, Columbia University, New York. Photo from the Library.

12. Frank R. Paul, illustration for Edmond Hamilton, 'Cities in the Air', cover illustration for *Air Wonder Stories,* November 1929. Jacques Sadoul Collection. All rights reserved.

13. 'Brantonne', cover for *Le Pionnier de l'atome,* by Jimmy Guieu. Paris: Éditions du Fleuve noir, 1952. La Maison d'ailleurs, Yverdon-les-Bains. Photo Flammarion.

14. Woolley, *Wonder Book of Aircraft,* 1931. Photo Mary Evans Picture Library, London.

15. Frank R. Paul, illustration for 'A Modern Atlantis', by F. Arthur Hodge, *Amazing Stories Quarterly,* spring 1928. All rights reserved.

16. Harvey Wiley Corbett, Towers on one of the Hudson Bridges in around 1975, drawing, *c.* 1930. Avery Architectural and Fine Arts Library, Columbia University, New York. Photo from the Library.

17. Frank R. Paul, illustration for 'Voice of Atlantis', by Laurence Manning, cover illustration for *Wonder Stories,* July 1934. Science Fiction Foundation, Essex. Photo Bernard Peek.

18. Guy Sabran, *La Rue de l'an 2000,* magazine illustration, 1934. Photo Mary Evans Picture Library.

19. Dick Calkins, *Buck Rogers in the 25th Century, c.*1934. All rights reserved.

20. Frank R. Paul, illustration for 'The Cubic City', Louis Tucker, *Science Wonder Stories,* September 1929. Photo Michael Dyer Associates Ltd., London.

21. Still from *Metropolis,* directed by Fritz Lang, Germany, 1926, based on the novel by Thea von Harbou. Photo Bildarchiv Preussischer Kulturbesitz, Berlin.

22. Hugh Ferriss, Apartment buildings built on a bridge, charcoal drawing, *c.*1925. Avery Architectural and Fine Arts Library, Columbia University, New York. Photo from the Library.

23. Leo Morey, illustration for 'Thia of the Dryland', by Harl Vincent, cover illustration for *Amazing Stories,* July 1932. Photo The Picture Library, Reed Consumer Books, London.

24. Frank R. Paul, 'City of the Future', cover illustration for *Amazing Stories,* April 1942. Cabinet des Estampes (Tb 971 p.12), Bibliothèque Nationale, Paris. Photo B. N.

25. Frank R. Paul, '10,000 Years Hence, A Prediction', *Air Wonder Stories,* November 1929. All rights reserved.

26. 'The Reader Speaks, A Department for SF Fans', *Thrilling Wonder Stories,* February 1952. All rights reserved.

27. Elliot Dold, illustration for 'Little Hercules', by Neil R. Jones, *Astounding Science Fiction,* September 1936. All rights reserved.

Chapter 4

1. Still from *Metropolis,* directed by Fritz Lang, Germany, 1926, based on the novel by Thea von Harbou. Photo Collection La Cinémathèque Française, Paris.

2. Elliot Dold, illustration for 'The Mightiest Machine', by John W. Campbell, *Astounding Stories,* December 1934. Science Fiction Foundation, Essex. Photo Bernard Peek.

3. Henri Lanos, 'L'Aéro-bagne 32', *Lectures pour tous,* September 1920. Département des Imprimés (8°Z 14580, p. 1660) Bibliothèque Nationale, Paris. Photo B. N.

4. Hugh Ferriss, *Steel,* charcoal drawing, *c.*1925. Avery Architectural and Fine Arts Library, Columbia University, New York. Photo from the Library.

5. Miller, illustration for 'I Tell You Three Times', Raymond F. Jones, cover illustration for *Astounding Science Fiction,* August 1951. La Maison d'ailleurs,Yverdon-les-Bains. Photo Flammarion.

6. Frank R. Paul, illustration for Philip F. Nowlan, 'Armageddon 2419 A.D.', *Amazing Stories,* August 1928. All rights reserved.

7. Howard V. Brown, illustration for 'Other Space', by Werner van Lorne, cover illustration for *Astounding Stories,* May 1937. Science Fiction Foundation, Essex. Photo Bernard Peek.

8. Still from *Metropolis,* directed by Fritz Lang, Germany, 1926, based on the novel by Thea von Harbou. Photo Collection La Cinémathèque Française, Paris.

9. Elliot Dold, illustration for 'The Machine', by Don A. Stuart, *Astounding Stories,* February 1935. Science Fiction Foundation, Essex. Photo Bernard Peek.

10. Pat Sullivan, Felix the Cat in the Year 2000, Paris, 1935. Cabinet des Estampes (Ka 73-6, 4° pp. 30, 31), Bibliothèque Nationale, Paris. Photo B. N.

11. Earle K. Bergey (?), cover illustration for *Captain Future, Man of Tomorrow,* autumn 1942. La Maison d'ailleurs, Yverdon-les-Bains. Photo Flammarion.

12. Wesso, illustration for 'After World's End', by Jack Williamson, cover illustration for *Marvel Science Stories,* February 1939. Photo Octupus Publishing, London.

13. Gordon Grant, illustration for *The Scarlet Plague,* by Jack London, London, 1912. Photo Michael Dyer Associates Ltd. London.

14. Henri Lanos, 'La Guerre future', *Je sais tout,* 15 March 1906. Département des Imprimés (8°Z 17063 p. 219) Bibliothèque Nationale, Paris. Photo B. N.

15. Cover illustration for *World War III,* March, 1950 (?). Photo Edimédia, Paris.

16. Brantonne, cover illustration for *Attentat cosmique,* by Jean-Gaston Vandel. Paris: Editions du Fleuve noir, 1953. La Maison d'ailleurs, Yverdon-les-Bains. Photo Flammarion

17. Howard V. Brown, illustration for 'Robot A-1', by Oscar J. Friend, cover illustration for *Startling Stories,* July 1939. Science Fiction Foundation, Essex. Photo Bernard Peek.

18. 'The "British Tar" of the Future', *Punch,* 1862. Photo Michael Dyer Associates Ltd. London.

19. Illustration for 'Earth's Friendly Invaders', cover illustration, *Strange Adventures,* July 1947. Photo Edimédia, Paris.

20. Joseph Hémard, illustration for *Nouveau code des impôts pour l'an fiscal 1995,* by Marcel Charpaux. Paris: Imprimerie E. Desfossées, 1947. La Maison d'ailleurs, Yverdon-les-Bains. Photo Flammarion.

21. Howard V. Brown, illustration for Stanley G. Weinbaum, 'The Black Flame', cover illustration for *Startling Stories,* January 1939. Science Fiction Foundation, Essex. Photo Bernard Peek.

22. Henri Lanos, illustration for 'When the Sleeper Wakes', by H. G. Wells, *The Graphic,* 21 January, 1899. Département des Imprimés, Bibliothèque Nationale, Paris. Photo B. N.

23. Charles Schneeman, illustration for 'To Follow Knowledge', *Astounding Science Fiction,* December 1942. Science Fiction Foundation, Essex. Photo Bernard Peek.

24. Edmund A. Emshwiller, illustration for 'The Defenders', by Philip K. Dick, cover illustration, *Galaxy Science Fiction,* January 1953. Jacques Sadoul Collection. All rights reserved.

25. Edmund A. Emshwiller, illustration for Jack Sharkey, 'The Programmed People', cover illustration for *Amazing Stories,* June 1963. La Maison d'ailleurs, Yverdon-les-Bains. Photo Flammarion.

26. Frank R. Paul, illustration for 'The Time Trap', by Henry Kuttner, cover illustration for *Marvel Science Stories,* November 1938. Science Fiction Foundation, Essex. Photo Bernard Peek.

27. Frank R. Paul, illustration for 'The Lord of Tranerica', by Stanton A. Coblentz, *Dynamic Science Stories,* February 1939. All rights reserved.

28. Ed Valigursky, illustration for 'The Iron Men of Venus', by Don Wilcox, *Amazing Stories,* February 1952. All rights reserved.

29. Bus, 'Aviation of the 21st Century', *Judge,* 1911. Photo Michael Dyer Associates, Ltd., London.

Chapter 5

1. Still, *Things to Come,* dir. by William Cameron Menzies, Great Britain, 1936, from the novel by H. G. Wells. All rights reserved.

2. Illustration for *Travel to Distant Worlds,* by Gilzin, Moscow, 1957. Photo Mary Evans Picture Library, London.

3. Still from *Destination Moon,* directed by Irving Pichel, United States, 1950. Photo Christophe L. Collection, Paris.

4. Frank R. Paul, illustration for 'Problems of Space Flying', by Herman Noordung, *Science Wonder Stories,* August 1929. Science Fiction Foundation, Essex. Photo Bernard Peek.

5. Frank R. Paul, illustration for 'Interplanetary Bridges', by Ludwig Anton, cover illustration for *Wonder Stories Quarterly,* winter 1933. All rights reserved.

6. Still from *Things to Come,* directed by William Cameron Menzies, Great Britain, 1936, based on the novel by H. G. Wells. Photo Collection La Cinémathèque Française, Paris.

7. Still from *Forbidden Planet,* directed by Fred McLeod Wilcox, United States, 1955. Photo Collection La Cinémathèque Française, Paris.

8. Still from *The Time Machine,* directed by George Pal, United States, 1959, based on the novel by H. G. Wells. Photo Christophe L. Collection, Paris.

9. Robert Gibson Jones, illustration for 'The Trail of the Astrogar', by Henry Hasse, cover illustration for *Amazing Stories,* October 1947. La Maison d'ailleurs, Yverdon-les-Bains. Photo Flammarion.

10. Raffin, illustration for *Voyage de cinq Américains dans les planètes,* by Henri de Graffigny, Paris, 1925 Département des Imprimés (4°Y2 6920 p. 197), Bibliothèque Nationale, Paris. Photo B. N.

11. Illustration for Hugo Gernsback, 'Ralph 124C 41+', *Modern Electrics,* 1911. All rights reserved.

12. *Tales of Tomorrow,* magazine cover illustration, *c.*1952. La Maison d'ailleurs, Yverdon-les-Bains. Photo Flammarion.

13. Hubert Rogers, illustration for 'Fury', by Henry Kuttner, cover illustration for *Astounding Science Fiction,* May 1947. Science Fiction Foundation, Essex. Photo Bernard Peek.

14. Frank R. Paul, illustration for Edmund Hamilton, 'The Eternal Cycle', cover illustration for *Wonder Stories,* March 1935. Jacques Sadoul Collection. All rights reserved.

15. Henri Lanos, illustration for 'La Fin du monde', by Camille Flammarion, *Je sais tout,* 15 Feb. 1905. Département des Imprimés (8°Z 17063 p. 55), Bibliothèque Nationale, Paris. Photo B. N.

16. Henri Lanos, illustration for 'La Fin du monde', by Camille Flammarion, *Je sais tout,* 15 February 1905. Département des Imprimés (8°Z 17063), Bibliothèque Nationale, Paris. Photo B. N.

17. Still from *When Worlds Collide,* directed by Rudolf Mare, United States, 1951. Photo PROD/DB.

18. Howard V. Brown (?), illustration for 'The Fortress of Utopia', by Jack Williamson, cover illustration for *Startling Stories,* Nov.1939. Science Fiction Foundation, Essex. Photo Bernard Peek.

19. Frank R. Paul, illustration for 'The Moon Doom', by Nathaniel Salisbury, cover illustration for *Wonder Stories,* February 1933. All rights reserved.

20. The Bomb, *World War III, c.*1950. Photo Édimédia, Paris.

21. Illustration for *L'Agonie du globe,* by Jacques Spitz, Paris, 1935. Photo Flammarion.

22. 'Captives of the Thieve-Star', cover illustration for *Planet Stories,* May 1951. Photo Octupus Publishing, London.

23. Still from the T.V. series *Star Trek,* United States, 1965. Photo Christophe L. Collection, Paris.

24. Alex Schomburg, cover illustration for *Amazing Stories,* February 1964. La Maison d'ailleurs, Yverdon-Les Bains. Photo Flammarion.

25. Still from *Flash Gordon,* directed. by Frederick Stephani and Ray Taylor, United States, 1936. Photo Christophe L. Collection, Paris.

26. Dick Calkins, *Buck Rogers in the 25th Century, c.*1934. All rights reserved.

27. Frank R. Paul, 'The Man from Mars', back cover illustration for *Fantastic Adventures,* May 1939. All rights reserved.

28. Frank R. Paul, 'The Man from Mars', back cover illustration for *Fantastic Adventures,* May 1939. All rights reserved

29. Interplanetary Voyage, box for a game, France. Photo Tapabor, Paris.

30. Frank R. Paul, 'Serenis, Water City of Callisto', back cover illustration for *Amazing Stories,* December 1941. La Maison d'ailleurs, Yverdon-les Bains. Photo Flammarion.

31. Frank R. Paul, illustration for 'Vandals of the Void', by J. M. Walsh, *Wonder Stories Quarterly,* summer 1931. All rights reserved.

Wake Me in a Thousand Years From Now

1. Still from *Things to Come,* directed by William Cameron Menzies, Great Britain, 1936, based on the novel by H. G Wells. All rights reserved.

2. Grandville, Pont enjambant les planètes, illustration for *Un autre monde,* 1844. Cabinet des Estampes (Tf 99b), Bibliothèque Nationale, Paris. Photo B. N.

Acknowledgements

The authors would like to express their gratitude
to everyone who has contributed assistance, advice, or access
to collections in the preparation of this book. Special thanks are due
to Roland Cléry, André-Clément Decouflé, Chantal Humbert,
Pascal Jean, Agnès Setton, François Mussard, Jacques Sadoul,
Pierre Versins and Alain Villemur.
The authors would also particularly like to thank
Julie, Laurence, Anne, Bernard, and Jean-Renaud
for their loyal and affectionate support.
Grateful acknowledgements and the authors' personal thanks
also go to all who gave permission for and assisted in the
reproduction of illustrations and pictures.
Sincere apologies are made to those who were not contacted
because addresses were inadequate or unknown,
with a hope for understanding and a request for contact so that
credit may be given in future editions.

Translated from the French by Francis Cowper
Copyediting by Patrick Hamm

Photographic research: Béatrice Petit

Design and typesetting: Anna Klykova, Atelier d'édition européen, Paris
Photoengraving: Bussière, Paris
Printed by: Clerc S.A., Saint-Amand-Montrond
Bound by: S.I.R.C., Marigny-le-Châtel

Flammarion
26, rue Racine 75006 Paris

ISBN : 2-08013-544-9
N° d'édition : 0657

Dépôt légal: September 1993

Printed in France